NEVEREST

MAXIM AND STEFAN IVANOV

NEVEREST

**4444 Nautical Miles, 105 Days in a Rowing Boat
Across the Atlantic in the Hurricane Season**

First published in Bulgaria in September 2021
by Vakon Publishing House

Cover design by Mira Minkova
Cover photos © Maxim and Stefan Ivanov
Inside photos © Maxim and Stefan Ivanov

Translated by © Christopher Buxton
Edited by Elena Mozsolics and Nicole Johnson
Editor-in-chief of Vakon Publishing House: Eleonora Gadjeva

Copyright © Vakon Publishing House

ISBN: 978-619-250-039-9

Dear readers,

You are holding in your hands a unique book. This is not only a tale of mutual love between father and son, of adventure, of strong spirit and unflinching determination. This is a book from which we can learn how to become good parents and how, with hard work, persistence, a positive attitude and mutual support, we can bring an idea to reality from its very conception, even without knowledge or experience.

Max and his family have been part of the St. George International School & Preschool community for the last 13 years. They are active participants in the life of the school and an example of all the values we share: honesty, responsibility, respect, initiative, mutual support, openness and tolerance. As parents, Jenny and Stefan have always supported both the school's and their children's initiatives.

Before our eyes, Max has developed not only as an excellent pupil, achieving high grades in his preparation for Cambridge A-level certificates and in the Bulgarian education program, but also as a responsible young person with a broad understanding of the world and his own contribution to society.

Max is a debating champion in the World Scholar's Cup and the Council of British International Schools Debating Competition, he has two certificates in the Guinness Book of World Records and together with his father, he won the competition for Man of the Year 2020 and, as will be proved, he is a talented writer.

We are so proud of Max and Stefan! What they have done and continue to do with their support for the cause Yes! To life! shows how everyone, as part of a supportive community – parents, relatives, friends, school – can set targets that at first sight seem unattainable and reach them, can develop themselves and others and realise their dreams.

We believe that we can expect yet more noble causes and achievements from Max and Stefan and from others, known and unknown, who have followed their example.

People like them bear an energy for change and they inspire us to become better people, better parents, better sons and daughters, and to change the world for the better.

Kremena Peneva and the whole team of
St. George International School and Preschool

www.stgeorgeschool.eu

Dear fellow pupils, teachers, staff and partners of St. George International School,

We are happy that we managed to realise our 'impossible dream'! Thank you for believing in us! You encouraged us and guided us and so from start to finish, we lived through the NEVEREST expedition across the Atlantic together.

Without the trust and support of my beloved school, in which I have had the joy to study at for 13 years now, this expedition would not have happened.

The freedom to express our ideas, even the craziest ones, our commitment and aspiration towards higher goals are at the root of St. George International School's spirit which each one of us carries within ourselves.

During our expedition, we realised that when you engage with a great challenge, many supporters emerge and with their help the impossible becomes possible. Thus, the path to the goal becomes easier and more realistic and friendships are created for life.

We wish that everyone realises their own small, big or 'impossible' dreams and we hope that one day, we ourselves can participate in the realisation of your boldest ideas.

With deepest respect,

Maxim   Stefan

When Stefan and Max shared their idea to cross the Atlantic in a rowing boat, they were hardly aware of the principal danger in this enterprise – the irreversible addiction to adventure that the ocean provides. It wasn't the navigational aids, but their dreams which turned into the compass that led them successfully through the elements.

Captain Valeri Petrov, NEVEREST
land based navigator

After many conversations with Max and Stefan, I met up with them in Portimão in Portugal in June 2020 when they were busy with the final preparations for their Atlantic crossing. They had built their own ocean rowing boat and were brimming with enthusiasm and positivity. I helped them with some last preparations before they set off very late in the season for a crossing that was going to be far from easy. It would be a trip, beset with equipment failure and weather conditions you don't wish for. Often I doubted that they would make it across, however the perseverance, strength and positivity of this father and son team, made them succeed in the middle of the hurricane season with a world record for Max as the youngest person ever to row across an ocean at the age of 16. The two are an inspiration for many people and their support for organ donation in Bulgaria met with enormous success.

I can't imagine that this will be their last adventure together!

Ralph Tuijn,
many times record holder
in ocean rowing;
NEVEREST land based navigator

When we talk excitedly about Max's and Stefan's ocean crossing adventure, the word we mention most often is 'record', but their achievement far, far exceeds the meaning. Records... Well, everyone has them in their lives, if they've put in just a little effort – in a national, world, or even in some neighbourhood competition. What happened in the summer of 2020 however, reported all over the world is much more than just a record. The NEVEREST expedition gave us a brilliant example of how an idea, vision and project can make a whole nation feel happy and motivated. There has not been such an event in Bulgaria's most recent history, and there's unlikely to be another such soon, although I'm an irredeemable optimist by nature.

Maxim Behar,
journalist and PR specialist

Bulgaria had not had a genuinely great marine achievement for many years before Max and Stefan brought about this ocean crossing, in whose success I never had any doubt. Perfect preparation, professionalism and good organisation are essential prerequisites for success and they carried them out in the best possible way.

Captain Nikolay Djambazov,
seafarer and author of
With Tangra Against the Wind

In life the majority of obstacles, trials and difficult lessons come unexpectedly, they challenge you to improvise based on your knowledge and experience, to give your very best, so as to overcome them and to continue... to the next lessons.

There are times too, when a person decides for themselves to leave their comfort zone, to look for situations, to prepare for them, to foresee them, to impatiently await their occurrence, so as to find out what they can bear and where their threshold of endurance lies.

I'm not going to compare one with the other. I'll only say that to be the latter, it's not necessary for you to be bored, to be mad, looking for the latest crazy idea to throw yourself into, or to be someone who wants to receive recognition for their egocentricity and recklessness. No, something else is needed. It's necessary to have a broad view of the world, to be brave and responsible, to be able to admit that you lack ability, but will do everything in your power to learn... to row, to build, to manage every challenge – from faulty equipment to horrifying hurricanes...

These two men proved that a man is as great as his dreams! And more – that the adventures we undertake give us the opportunity to see things from a different angle, equip us with new ideas, provoke us. They post innermost desires on the horizon, which we've yearned for, but for one reason or another, we've pushed to the bottom of our consciousness. Adventures are like punctuation marks in a book – without them everything would be stripped of emotion!

And despite the obstacles through which one has to get through, one has to carry on and to fight. Because that is happiness – the path to the achievement of the goal, the thrill which you experience in the meantime, and the achievement – that's just the cherry on the cake.

Victoria Dimitrova,
world champion rower and
Maxim's and Stefan's rowing trainer

CONTENTS

PART 1

PART 2

All growth starts at the end of your comfort zone.

Tony Robbins

As long as you live, keep learning how to live.

Lucius Seneca

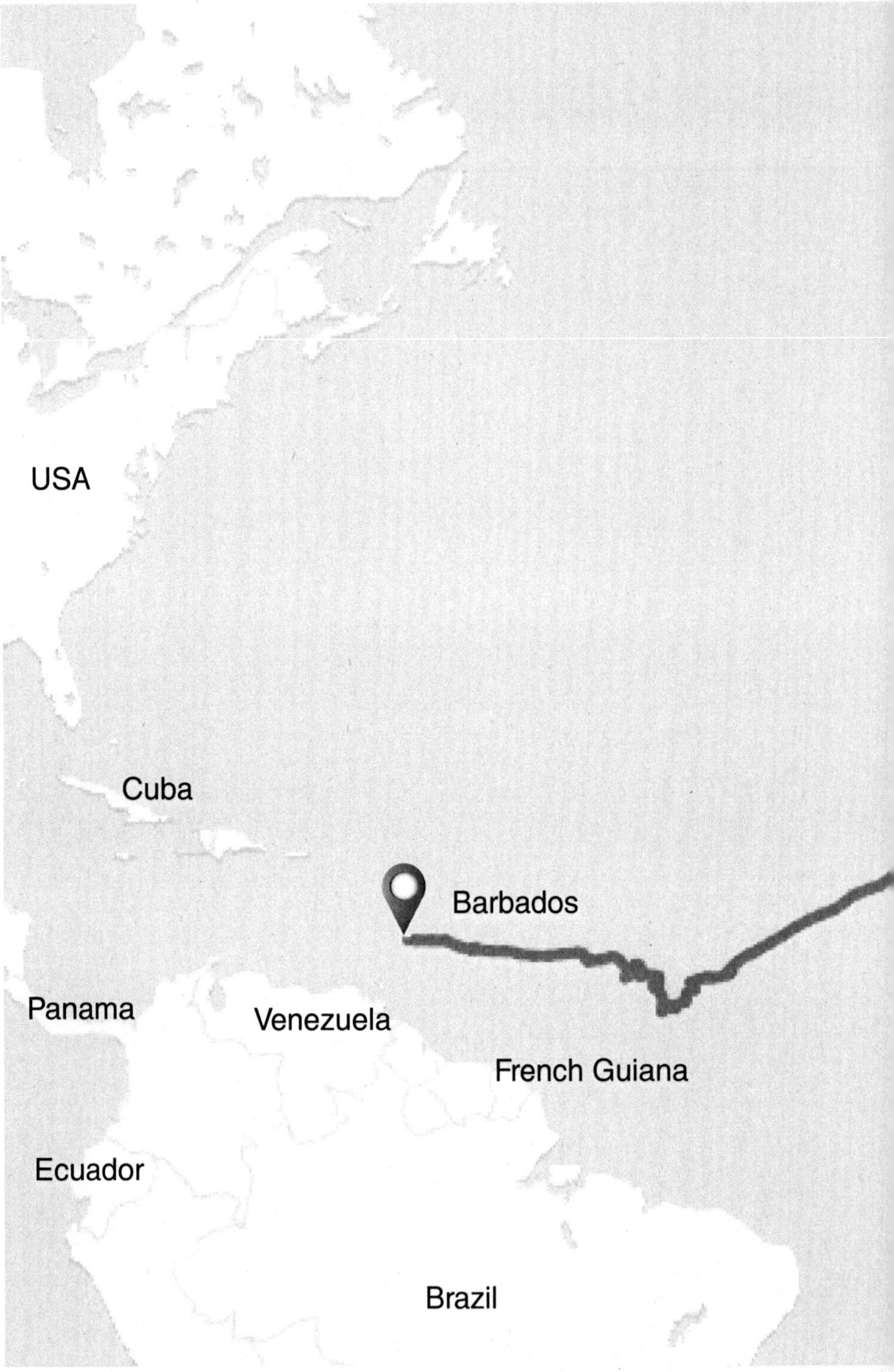
USA
Cuba
Barbados
Panama
Venezuela
French Guiana
Ecuador
Brazil

Great Britain

Germany

France

Italy

Bulgaria

Spain

Portugal

Morocco

Algeria

Libya

Lanzarote

Cape Verde

Mali

Niger

Senegal

Chad

Nigeria

Angola

PART 1

PREPARATION

Chapter 1

"Dad, someday you'll get to cross the Atlantic in a rowing boat!" I exclaimed one evening, as all my family were gathered round the dining table.

I saw the baffled looks from my mother Jenny and my sister Lara while on my father Stefan's face, a smile spread.

It was the autumn of 2018, I'd only just turned fifteen. Our family dinner followed its usual pattern, discussing everyday matters and making plans for the weekend. Nothing presaged the start of an unforgettable adventure.

The evening, though, was quite different from any other.

I'll go back a little in time, to share the fact that my father adores challenges. Although finance is his professional field, he's been a fan of extreme experiences since childhood. He likes to experiment with different kinds of sport – from skiing and snowboarding, surfing and windsurfing to Taekwondo and mountain-biking.

When he turned 39, he got into long-distance running and not only did he run marathons, but tried his strength in mountain ultramarathons. I've always been impressed by his insatiable appetite for big challenges. I remember how happy he was when he succeeded in finishing the Vitosha 100, took part in the Pirin Ultra (67 kilometres), ran in the Lavaredo Ultra (87 kilometres), the UTMB-PTL (300 kilometres), etc. In Copenhagen, he finished the Ironman which comprised a 3.8 kilometres swim, a 180 kilometres bicycle ride and a 42 kilometres run, in excellent time. Although he never trained in professional swimming, in 2011 he swam The English Channel and became the second Bulgarian to cross this stretch of water between England and France. The first, was the legendary swimming contestant Peter Stoychev who, for 11 successive years, led the world rankings for marathon swimming in open water.

Of course, I threw out the idea of rowing the Atlantic as a joke initially, thinking that to cross an ocean in a rowing boat was an absolutely impossible undertaking. In spite of this however, the thought of the challenge nibbled away at the corners of my subconscious and that very evening I sat down and searched the internet for more information. I found out that there were people who had crossed not just the Atlantic but other oceans too in rowing boats. This discovery was unexpected and both amazed and excited me. I wanted to find out more about these extreme rowers and their experiences.

That's how I found out about the Dutchman Ralph Tuijn, who on his own and with other rowers had carried out nine expeditions across the Atlantic, Pacific and Indian Oceans. On one of these, on the 26th of

January 2015, he set out in a rowing boat from Lagos, Portugal and reached Cedros, Trinidad and Tobago. There were four other rowers participating in the expedition: Sam Greatrix, Tara Adams, Jim Alsford and Nicholas Sen. They crossed the Atlantic Ocean in 52 days and 6 hours, during which they managed to set a record for the fastest Atlantic crossing from Europe to South America, as before finishing their voyage in Trinidad and Tobago they touched on the Venezuela coast.

I came across the story of the Canadian, Mylène Paquette who managed a solo crossing of the North Atlantic. She set out on the 6th of July 2013 from Halifax, Canada and reached Lorient, France in 128 days and 22 hours. Thus, she became the first person from the Americas to successfully row solo across the North Atlantic. For 45 of the first 60 days of the expedition, the weather and navigational conditions were so bad that Mylène was forced to remain in the cabin, while the boat was held by a drogue anchor.

I admit that I was really surprised to learn, not only that there had been such expeditions, but all the details about them; such an undertaking seemed to me exceptionally difficult, almost superhuman. As I read the stories of these brave voyagers, I felt simultaneously afraid and attracted towards such an unimaginable adventure. I pictured how we would row for thousands of miles, a team, father and son, roaming across the endless ocean, relying only on our own strength and sometimes on luck and the weather's benevolence. I was in awe of everything that remained to be learnt, of the difficulties that I'd have to face and try to overcome. Before my eyes a new world opened up, linked to navigation, to the seas and their inhabitants, and the exceptional opportunity to get to know our strengths and weaknesses.

I could not stop surfing the sea of information regarding these voyages. Ocean rowing boats were festooned with all kinds of antennas, satellite and navigational devices and looked more like spaceships than ordinary boats, which was fascinating. Some rowers had crossed the oceans solo and others in teams of two, three or even six. The stories they told were exciting and seemed genuine, unforgettable and unrepeatable. I wanted to feel and live through something as exceptional, and this sparked the adventurer in me.

There was no need for long deliberation or anyone to convince us, my father and I quickly decided we would not only row across the Atlantic together, but we would construct the boat ourselves. That way we would know exactly how it had been built and how strong it was, as well as gain experience of boatbuilding and seafaring, which would all be invaluable to us on the ocean. We did not underestimate the thousands of hours we would be working on the boat together which would also help us become a better team.

My summers up to this moment had been like those of a typical teenager: I adored going to the seaside, seeing friends and cousins, travelling through Bulgaria and sometimes abroad, mostly with my parents and sister, occasionally without my family. What perhaps sets me aside is the fact that I believed in myself and in my ability to overcome all sorts of obstacles, whatever they may be. I think people limit themselves too much and set up invisible barriers to achieving their dreams. That summer I had no clue I would be setting out on a long and boundless journey, but having accepted the idea I was ready for the challenge of escaping everyday monotony.

My paternal grandfather Nikolay, had been a Master of Sports in gymnastics and a professor of mechanical engineering in the Higher Institute of Mechanical and Electrical Engineering (currently the Technical University) in Sofia. There he met my grandmother, Karina, a student in electrical engineering. I believe this may explain our natural ability to construct machines, adapt vehicles, build electrical systems and take on any kind of engineering challenge.

We began to dream, to plan and to debate, we undertook serious research to learn as much as we possibly could about such an undertaking and to minimise the chance of nasty surprises. We discovered that about a third of ocean crossing attempts in a rowing boat were unsuccessful. Despite unearthing such worrying statistics of failure, we were not deterred. On the contrary, we found the idea more compelling even though the thought of crossing the ocean in a small rowing boat was terrifying. After more delving, we found out that of the several hundred rowing boats daring to embark on ocean voyages, only eight had lost rowers at sea and only two of them had more than one rower on board. One of the boats had six rowers – one of whom had fallen overboard, never to be found; the other lost its pair of rowers – the only boat that had lost more than one person. This had happened however, in 1966, more than half a century ago, when communication and navigation technologies were of a much lower standard.

We were already convinced that without a suitable boat, we'd get nowhere so our time and energy had to be concentrated on the building phase; we would plan the voyage once this had been achieved. This decision brought me relief in the moments when I worried how we would manage the challenge, whether it was too much of a risk or just downright crazy. Deep down inside I knew that we would do everything possible to guarantee our personal safety and the success of the voyage.

FIRST STEPS
17 SEPTEMBER 2018, STEFAN

When in the course of the family dinner Max 'threw down the gauntlet' of a rowing boat Atlantic crossing, the first thought that passed through my mind was: "Wow, what a great challenge!"

From the time when Max and Lara were quite small, I've striven to stimulate them into seeking out activities that would engage their thinking and creativity and develop them as individuals. I avoided slapping an immediate veto when one of them wanted to sleep in a tent in the mountains with their friends or learn how to snowboard. Rather, along with them, we would think through the idea and whether it was a good one and how to realise it in the most reasonable way. At first, Jenny and Lara didn't take the idea seriously but Max and I got down to carefully researching the topic and once we established that such ocean rowing expeditions are possible and very rarely end fatally for the crew, and after lengthy discussions with several ocean rowers, the decision was taken to undertake the voyage.

At first, we didn't know where to start. I wanted Max and I to construct the boat ourselves, to demonstrate that it is possible to build something with your own hands, even if you have no experience in the specific field. I hoped that this would give Max more confidence and show him that when you apply your energy and dedication to something, you can indeed succeed. Moreover, in this way, we would get to know every element of the boat's construction and be able to repair it if it broke down or suffered damage during the voyage. During the construction process we would spend hundreds, even thousands of hours together, which these days rarely happens between a father and his teenage son. There's no doubt, we would bump into really difficult stages in the creation of the boat and even more serious and stressful moments during the voyage, which would take at least a month, perhaps two or three, however this would make the whole experience even more exciting and rewarding. I strongly believed these efforts and difficulties would temper the steel in Max's character and would be useful to him later in life, whatever professional path he chose to follow. Competition in every field is becoming more global and merciless and to succeed, you have to apply a combination of hard work, ingenuity and courage. I hoped he would be able to learn many useful lessons from the expedition, regardless of whether it was successful or not.

As we lacked experience and knowledge in boatbuilding, we feared that if we designed it on our own, there was a real possibility the boat would be too narrow, which would make the inboard oar-shaft too short and rowing very hard. On the other hand, if it were too wide that would be dangerous because if waves capsized it, it would not self-right. Other possibilities were that it might sit too low in the water, which would allow waves to regularly inundate the boat; or that it might sit too high, which would cause serious rocking and make rowing very difficult.

We decided, therefore, that the sensible thing would be to find one of the best designers of ocean rowing boats and purchase plans for a two person boat which we would then build on our own in our family garage. It turned out that the English boat designer Phil Morrison, had drawn up the blueprints for more than three quarters of all the ocean rowing boats in recent years.

There was no doubt as to Phil's expertise and authority in this field, as nearly all speed records and first voyages had been established in boats he had designed. He was our man.

It wasn't at all easy to get in contact with him though, as he had no social media profile, website or contact details in the yellow pages. Fortunately, we found out that he used to be an associate member of the Pevensey Bay Yacht Club on the English south coast and sent them an email on the 17th of September 2018, with a plea to put us in contact with him. The Club responded to our email and in a couple of days we were chatting to Phil on the phone.

We told him about our dream of building an ocean rowing boat in our garage and that we had no experience of rowing and ocean voyages. He let us know that at this point in time he was considering retiring and withdrawing from active work with boats and competitions. He made it clear that in order to help us, it would not be enough to send designs of boats he had drawn up previously as they had been prepared with specialised shipyards in mind, equipped with vacuum machines for applying the resins and special moulds. This would not be practical in the building of one single boat in our garage.

During the course of our conversations Phil must have become aware of our enormous desire to realise our dream, or perhaps our despair about not managing without his help, because ultimately he agreed to draw up and send us an authentic design of an ocean rowing boat that we could build in a domestic setting. We were amazed that he entertained two absolute beginners and agreed to help us without being sure we wouldn't change our minds the next day!

We agreed the design would cost a modest sum, since Phil reasoned he would be able to sell the project to other enthusiasts afterwards. Several weeks later we received the first draft designs and to be honest, we didn't like them, despite knowing nothing of boat construction. The boat seemed too big and it had an aft cabin which seemed too small for two people. It took some courage to share our concerns with Phil, especially as we had never actually set foot in an Olympic rowing boat, but luckily , Phil readily admitted that the design was based on archaic models he had used in the past, and agreed to design something more modern and functional especially for us. The second design he sent us had a bow cabin, but it was surrounded by a deck gunwale which made the cabin smaller and the boat look more like a fishing vessel than a sports one. Fortunately, Phil agreed to correct this design as well, to get rid of the gunwale around the cabin and send us a third variant (see figure 1), which we immediately fell in love with. The boat resembled an American war plane made with "Stealth" technology, which had a pared down design with sharp curves developed to reach supersonic speeds. It looked like a futuristic machine from another planet!

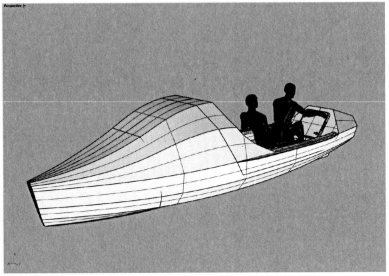

Fig. 1 The final design of our boat created by Phil Morrison

A DO IT YOURSELF ON TWO WHEELS
STEFAN

The boat wasn't the first vehicle which Max and I had constructed in our garage. When he was eight or nine years old, we decided to fulfil one of my childhood dreams and make a motorbike out of spare parts – like the Lego models Max liked to put together. The bike was in the style of a chopper – similar to a Harley Davidson, but with its 2400 cc engine, looked more like its bigger brother. In comparison, it was as powerful as 48 Balkan bikes (Balkan was the first motorbike I'd ridden as a child) and 2.4 times bigger than an engine of a car like a Volkswagen Polo, for example.

We chose specific models among engines from Ultima, frames from Sander Motorcycle Works, carburettors from S&S, etc. and ordered them from the USA. The back tyre which we decided on for the bike was 30 centimetres wide – a lot wider than a car tyre. The electrical system consisted of dozens of multi-coloured cables, which had to be built into the frame. We had such boyish fun in the garage and felt like inventors. Max had his specific tasks, which he had to carry out without my help, for example, mounting the headlight on the bike. Sometimes I scratched my head over how to install certain parts, as we had no instruction booklet for every step of the construction. When the moment came to push the starter button, I felt an excitement, similar to that when Max and Lara were born. We had to change the configuration of the cables three times as the first two attempts yielded no signs of life. The third time however, it started up and the rumble and thunderous clatter of the engine was so strong that if we'd had amalgam fillings they'd have surely fallen out on the first ride.

Well, our fillings didn't fall out, but the first trips with the bike were solo, until I made sure that everything was working as it should. The bike had some teething problems: sometimes, due to the vibration, this or that bolt would fall off, along with the part it was supporting. I had to use a special glue for the bolts and nuts, to eliminate this problem. After riding several hundred kilometres however, the engine stabilised and to this very day – almost ten years later – it continues to work with minimal faults. To my regret no one in my family shows any desire to ride with me on the bike. Every time I invite them, they turn me down with some excuse – that it was too noisy, that it is going to rain, etc.

Constructing a boat is not an easy undertaking and is not like assembling ready made parts. You have to build the body, the deck, the storage compartments, the cabin, etc. from scratch. It's essential to apply exceptional precision in the construction of the designed hydro and aerodynamic shapes and ensure they are strong enough to withstand ocean storms. You have to select and install navigation and communication devices, equipment which is used in rescue operations, and to take care of dozens of details, which are essential for the survival of ocean voyagers. We had no idea what materials and tools to use or how to handle them. Therefore, once again we decided to seek the help of experts in the relevant fields and to benefit from their experience and knowledge. It would have been a huge waste of time and resources 'to reinvent the wheel' in every field.

We contacted Captain Nikolay Djambazov – the great Bulgarian seafarer who built his own yacht, Tangra and completed a round the world voyage, passing Cape Horn, with it in 1983. Apart from Tangra he had built and restored many other sea going vessels and completed dozens of voyages across seas and oceans. From his book With Tangra against the Wind, we not only gained inspiration about what a man can achieve, but also learnt some important lessons about seafaring. Captain Djambazov, from our first meeting, made us understand that sailing the ocean is a serious and dangerous business and that we could not possibly imagine what we had undertaken. When we asked him a question related to seafaring, his answer was always based on his personal experience of years spent building and sailing sea vessels across seas and oceans. He gave us instructions on how to manage in bad weather – to run downwind and tie the drogue anchor out from the stern, even if this resulted in a temporary divergence from the course we've set. He told us about the breaking waves, about the unpredictable situations which would surely develop during our expedition and about what a potentially insurmountable mental challenge a long sea voyage might have on the mind of a sixteen year old youth.

In spite of all the warnings and stories he shared with us, Nikolay Djambazov wanted to help us and immediately put us in touch with his friend, engineer Stoyan Voivodov, who agreed to give us practical guidance on the construction of the boat. To understand what kind of man Stoyan is, it has to be noted that he is the first Bulgarian to have had the courage to build his own hang glider and fly with it. In fact Stoyan made a number of better and better hang glider variants, the first of which he built from a photograph measuring 4x4 centimetres from the Paralleli magazine, extrapolating the hang glider measurements according to their proportions to the assumed size of the pilot, flying it. Following this, Stoyan took part in hang glider competitions and won several of them. His way of flying a hang glider was more innovative than was typical at that time. Instead of plotting a straight line from the start to the finish, as most of his fellow competitors did, he would analyse the winds in advance so he could use them effectively during the flight to carry him to his goal at maximum speed.

Stoyan had made a number of catamarans and boats from fibreglass in his garage and had accumulated extensive experience in building such vessels in domestic conditions. He had experimented with the widest range of resins and fillers, wood sheeting and special cores, stainless steel fastenings, etc. We told him that we didn't want him to help us physically in the building of our boat, just to give us advice, so that we could succeed in building it on our own. Stoyan took our dream to heart and not only gave us directions for each construction stage, but out of his private stores, he shared with us the best quality materials that he'd discovered and tested – epoxy resins and fillings, light porous cores with cells like those of a honeycomb, strand mat and fibreglass cloth, etc. Stoyan liked to join us in head-scratching to find solutions for the different stages of construction and he'd always come up with alternative ideas through the course of hours, or even minutes.

When I return to the beginning of our adventure, I have to admit that we met people who, just like us, set themselves seemingly impossible goals but did not give up their pursuit. I realised that we wouldn't have achieved either the construction of a motorbike or boat or the transoceanic crossing, if I hadn't been taught by my family that one should never give in to boredom and become lazy, that even a child should be able to cope with challenges and that, as we help each other, life becomes happier. These are lessons I'll remember all my life and which have helped me when I am faced with difficulty or I have a moment's hesitation.

When I was eight years old, I lived through a very difficult moment. My father Nikolay died from a brain tumour. There followed several years in which my mother Karina had to bring my sister and I up on her own. Fortunately, from time to time, we could rely on help from our Grannie Emilia and Granddad Kolyo. Later on my mother married my wonderful, devoted stepfather Ognyan whose son, Kalin became our much-loved brother and we lived once again as one happy family. My mother never dropped her head and never allowed life's battles to crush her. From early childhood, she encouraged us to try out new interests and didn't try to stop me when I got obsessed with motorbikes or when I decided to leave home and study abroad. From an early age, I've loved challenges and I deliberately seek them out – that's how I get more fun out of life. When I've succeeded in the latest challenge, irrespective of whether it was educational, intellectual, professional or sporting, I experience the sweetest feeling – fulfilment.

Max and I told my mother that we were building a boat and were thinking of crossing the ocean with it, and rather than dissuading us, she began to help in whatever way she could. She found all kinds of things that could be useful like, for example, an especially absorbent cloth, which we could wet and tie round our necks, to keep us cool in the burning sun. She gently conveyed her motherly words of wisdom and tried her best not to look worried, so as not to cause us unnecessary concern.

I'll never forget the support which my mother gave me in all the big challenges throughout my life. I felt her love and strength and this has helped me overcome the most serious obstacles that faced me.

One such moment was my decision to go to study in an American university.

I graduated from the American University in Sofia with a BA in Business Administration; my next goal was to obtain a Masters in the USA. I shared my plans with my mother, telling her that I'd try to get a scholarship. She stood behind my decision, encouraging me to try and she gave me all her savings which were the equivalent of 300 dollars.

It was in the middle of the 1990s – the most poverty stricken years in Bulgaria. Hyperinflation had melted the value of people's savings and the market economy couldn't work to expectations. It was hard, as much for my family as for the whole of society, but I had my own plans and was ready to follow them. I wanted to get my MBA in Finance and I applied to 16 US universities in the hope of not just being accepted, but being offered a scholarship, because the annual tuition fee at those universities was around 20,000 dollars – more than my mother had earned in her life up to this moment.

Over the course of months I researched universities on the other side of the ocean, corresponded with them by mail, requested application fee waivers, wrote various essays, filled in countless forms, and underwent tests. In the end, 12 universities accepted me and four of these offered me almost full scholarships. I chose to study at Cornell University which is situated in the city of Ithaca, in New York State. Cornell was founded in 1865 by Ezra Cornell and Andrew Dixon White and is a member of the Ivy League, a group of eight elite universities in the US. Cornell did not offer me a scholarship, but I managed to get by somehow, by working part time at four places while I studied. I was a teaching assistant to the Entrepreneurship Professor, David Ben Daniel as well as his research assistant helping him with the book he was writing about international mergers and acquisitions; I taught statistics lessons as a private tutor; and I was a resident assistant at one of the university residence halls. When I talk of the sweet feeling of fulfilment, I have in mind the feeling after you have worked almost around the clock for three years – including the application process and the two years at Cornell. The time spent at the university and my life in the United States gave me the confidence to believe I could cope with anything, if I applied the necessary energy and didn't give up. And this is what I also want to impart to my children.

Chapter 2

A CONFIDENT START
18 OCTOBER 2018, MAX

On the evening of the 18th of October, we had a party at our house to celebrate my mother's birthday which is on the 16th. The party was approaching its end and so we asked the men, before they left, to come down to the garage and help us move a five metre wooden board, weighing more than 300 kilograms. We put it on blocks of parquet tiles, so we could begin the boat building on top of it. We'd brought this board, made from Angelim wood from the Dinezia Excelsa tree, from Brazil, in order to fashion it into a family dining table; but up until now we had only used it for the construction of the motorbike.

After we'd put it over the blocks, the board looked to me like an empty white page, over which you might ponder the writing of a book. Everything depended on us, on our determination and imagination. I wanted us to create something we'd remember all our lives and which we'd be really proud of. The bare surface was a little daunting because I imagined how out of nothing we were about to build a six to seven-metre long boat. It was a pivotal moment of realisation, the beginning of something huge and exceptional; I knew that we had sufficient zeal to succeed, no matter how much hard work and preparation it would take. I was pleased we got organised and didn't get lost from the word go, before deciding where to start.

We found a printing firm which would print out on paper the panels for the hull, the cabin, the bulkheads and the deck, with the real measurements of the boat. We then cut them with scissors while contemplating how we could render the paper patterns into the contours of the boat, over the board in the garage. This was a challenge, given that the hull of the boat was not flat but rounded both length and width-wise.

After considerable thought and discussion, we decided to install two aluminium seven metre rails over the board, to fasten them tight, set at one metre apart, and over these we began to put in place temporary chipboard panels with the shapes of the bulkheads which Phil Morrison had designed. Later we'd have to exchange these for the permanent bulkheads of fibreglass, so that they would ensure a strong internal structure to the boat. Because each of the bulkheads had a different shape and was positioned at a different height relative to the waterline in both its top and bottom parts, we needed to work out how to approach their construction. It took us some time to come up with the solution; we decided it would be easier to fasten them to the rails, by casting an imaginary plane parallel to the waterline, which would divide the bulkheads into two parts. We cut the parts of the bulkheads lying under this imaginary plane out of chipboard and fastened them upside down to the rails; those parts which had to be fixed to the bottom of the boat would be sticking up in the air. It was as if we were building the boat upside down with the hull at the top. Three of the bulkheads had to be positioned vertically – perpendicular to the waterline, and the remaining four – at different angles to it. Instead of trying to hit the accurate angles under which we'd have to fasten the cut bulkheads, we measured down to the millimetre the distance between the bulkheads in Phil's drawings both at their lowest and their highest points. With the help of small aluminium fasteners, we attached the bulkheads to the rails, keeping to these measurements.

For the first time, we bought and began to use a tool called a rivet gun, with which we installed rivets instead of bolts. Thus, we easily fixed the aluminium fasteners to each other and to the chipboard bulkheads. As the distance between each two bulkheads was about a metre, if we had tried to build the hull from fibreglass directly over them, it would not have been possible to achieve a smooth curved shape of the hull. There would certainly have been creases where the bulkheads were and flatter parts of the hull between them, which would create a huge resistance in the boat's passage through the water. That is why we bought long and thin aluminium profiles and fastened them over the temporary bulkheads – from first to last (from the prow to the stern), so that these profiles – stringers – would shape the curved boat's hull. Over them, with the help of the rivet gun, we attached temporary panels which we cut from plywood using the paper shapes. So we achieved something like a mould in the shape of the boat's hull, turned upside down over the wooden board in the garage. Fortunately, we avoided losing any fingers in the process as this was also the first time we had used a jigsaw which looked like my mother's iron but with a small saw blade jutting from the base, which moved up and down faster than the eye could follow. At the beginning I avoided using it, however my father took up the task with relish.

Following Stoyan's advice, we put a thin nylon over the temporarily constructed body of the hull and began to lay over it thin six-millimetre panels, of a material similar to plastic, which he had given us. These panels were to serve as the core for the boat's final construction from fibreglass. The nylon was necessary so the epoxy resin we planned to laminate with, would not stick the core panels to the plywood. We cut out panels, using the same paper shapes, and literally sewed them one to the other with a crooked needle and thread. Each core panel was incredibly light, looked like a thin honeycomb with tiny cells and was extremely porous, so that the epoxy resin was absorbed into it – resulting in a strong hard wall of the correct shape. We didn't worry too much about the weight of the boat as we assumed there was no way it could end up being too heavy. These were sadly only presumptions associated with the initial stage of the work, before the laminating process began. In due course, we realised that we actually should have been concerned about the boat's weight.

We shaped the boat's prow separately from a thick insulation panel with the help of a knife and rasp. While working on this part I felt like a sculptor, carving out his first statue. The work was precise and required full concentration. The boat's prow was narrower at its base and a lot wider at its top and we had to render by hand the three-dimensional oval shape over which we'd later apply the fibreglass. It was neither boring nor tiring, rather it was creative and one of the most pleasurable procedures of the boat's construction. During this process, I began to feel what it means to create something unique with one's own hands, applying effort, patience and creativity.

LAMINATING AND MEDITATION
2 JANUARY 2019, STEFAN

The hours, the days, the months passed by unnoticed. The time spent in the garage; the plans and conversations with Max; the building of the boat; they filled me with joy. I experienced fully, every small step and every success that would lead us to the start of our voyage. After the first stages in the boat's planning and creation, the moment came to start laminating. Yet another process which we knew nothing about and we were about to learn. We carefully mastered the finer points from Stoyan, as he systematically led us through the process. In the evening, we sat and watched video clips on the internet, in order to confirm what we had learnt and compare different techniques. Before starting the actual work, it was extremely important to buy appropriate quality materials and as a result of conversations with Stoyan we armed ourselves with a long list which included:

- Epoxy resin and hardener. According to most of the specialists, the recommendation was to choose epoxy, and not a cheaper polyester material, which is used in the construction of some boats.

- Strand mat (filaments of fibreglass, stuck one over the other, which sometimes get unstuck and pierce the skin, until they are smothered in resin) and fibreglass cloth (a thicker textile, woven from braided fibres which ensures the strength of the fibreglass structure).
- Paint brushes, with which to spread the resin over every layer of fibreglass or strand mat and an aluminium roller, with which to press every new layer so as not to leave miniature air bubbles in the resin.
- A special powder like filler to mix with the resin, so it becomes as dense as plasticine, with which to glue the bulkheads to the hull and, all in all, stick every fibreglass component, one to the other.
- Koreselin, with which to clean the tools and thin out the resin.
- Gas masks with special filters, to protect our lungs from poisonous gases emitted from the resins, when they are mixed with hardeners and from the Koreselin vapour
- Latex gloves and plastic bags, to help protect ourselves and the garage from resin splashes.

The actual laminating process comprised the application of a coat of resin, the positioning of either strand mat or fibreglass fabric over it, the spreading of yet another layer of resin and the pressing out of any bubbles with the aluminium roller. Every piece of strand mat or fibreglass was cut out, so as to cover one panel entirely and to re-cover a few centimetres of all the neighbouring panels. The application of each layer over each panel took several hours. After we'd applied a layer over a given panel, we had to wait 24 hours for the resin to harden, after which we returned again to the garage and applied a layer of strand mat or fibreglass fabric to the neighbouring panels, so that the layers covered each other, gaining maximum strength.

In order to achieve the construction of a fibreglass type sandwich, we laminated the outside wall of the hull with five to seven coats of resin using successive strips of strand mat and fibreglass; and the interior sides of the hull, as well as both sides of the deck, with three to five layers of strand mat and fibreglass fabric. We made the bulkheads from two layers of core, laminating each of them from both sides with up to three layers of strand mat and fibreglass fabric, and after that we glued them together.

My daughter Lara, my nephew Nikola Dimitrov and one of Max's best friends, Alex Denchev, sometimes came to help with the laminating of various parts of the boat. I enjoyed observing the youngsters as they tried to manage the task with care and precision. The whole laminating process carried on for more than two months, over which time various parts of my body were regularly itching from the fibreglass filaments which easily penetrated the skin. In the end, I had an allergic reaction to the fibreglass – the skin on the inside of my forearm became inflamed, dried up and flaked. It wasn't a great sensation, but I accepted it as one of the stages of endurance necessary to achieve our goal!

In spite of some discomfort, I discovered that the working process of repeating the same actions over and over, like spreading, sticking, pressing out bubbles, etc. was deeply relaxing and had a good effect on my psyche and concentration. It was as if I was meditating several hours a day, almost every day. I wore a gas mask with a special filter so I don't believe the feeling of release and self-absorption was caused by intoxication of the gases emitted by the epoxy resins. With every layer applied, I felt that we were getting ever closer to the day of the launch and this brought about little doses of satisfaction. It seemed to me that the contours of the boat we were sculpting out of fibreglass were truly wonderful. Of course, they were not perfectly smooth or symmetrical but they possessed the charm of a handcrafted home-made creation, and not a factory produced element coming out of a mould.

After we finished with the application of strand mat and fibreglass fabric, we made up a thick paste of epoxy resin and filler-powder and spread it with a spatula in layers over the hull. We waited for every layer to harden and smoothed it with electric sanders, so as to achieve a surface as smooth as possible – a process which took longer than a day's work after the application of each layer. There was no way the surface would be perfect, however hard we tried, and whatever time we devoted to sanding down. The epoxy powder flew everywhere and filled the whole place. It stuck to the walls, floor and ceiling, so we were always careful to wear special masks to prevent breathing this dust into our lungs. The last stage of laminating consisted of covering the hull with two coats of a mixture of 90% epoxy resin and 10% Koreselin to achieve a water-resistant surface. This stage was exceptionally important for the safety of our voyage.

The time came to fix the permanent fibreglass bulkheads to the hull of the boat. We did this, using a thick paste prepared from epoxy resin, mixed in with strand mat fibres and a powdery filler. Lara again decided to put on a gas mask, roll up her sleeves and help us with this tricky task. The thick paste looked like the plasticine she'd loved to play with a lot as a child. I remember how she spent hours sculpting little figures from soft plasticine and afterwards telling us all stories about them. Suddenly the construction of the boat turned into a game, in which old and young discovered something interesting for themselves. For me, the knowledge that all of my family were, in one way or another, taking part in the boat's creation meant a great deal. In every following step I felt the strong support from those closest to me; their desire to help in the realisation of a dream.

We divided the boat into 13 waterproof compartments, so that if any of them leaked and flooded, the rest would remain dry and keep the boat afloat. One of these sections was the cabin in which we would sleep; the rest were larger or smaller holds for food, anchors, spare parts, safety vests and anything else we might need on the boat. Among the stories of narrow escapes with ocean rowing boats, we came across a picture of a boat which had been pierced during the voyage by a swordfish – part of the sword remained stuck into the hull. We hoped that if we did a good job, such incidents would not put an end to our voyage.

One of our more serious concerns before the launch was the fear that a great storm would toss the boat from wave to wave, bashing and sweeping over it, causing it to break up and fill with water. This is the reason we assiduously applied layer after layer of fibreglass and did not stint with the coats of resin, to ensure our boat was as strong as possible.

In some places where strength was of critical importance, we embedded additional support, plugging three-millimetre thick pieces of stainless steel (AISI 316 recommended for the sea) between the layers of fibreglass. Such places were the gunwales on both sides, into which would be bolted the plates for the swivelling oarlocks which would hold the oars; the stern where the rudder is fixed to the boat; the hull behind the U-bolts, to which we'd tie the ropes to the drogue anchors or to towing boats; and the cleats, around which we'd tie our boat to quays or to other boats. We feared that if the gunwale broke where the oarlock was or the U-bolt that held the drogue anchor broke from the prow, we wouldn't be able to complete the voyage and therefore we tried to make these parts so strong that practically the whole boat could hang off them.

Phil had told us that it is better to be sure the boat is strong and to sleep soundly, rather than make it as light as possible in order to have a greater chance of breaking a speed record for an ocean crossing, and to have the constant worry of it rupturing. Following this advice, we may have overdone the layers of fibreglass and the steel plates. The boat became more solid, like a capsule from a space rocket in which the astronauts landed back on Earth, than the light racing rowing boats we'd seen on Pancharevo Lake, which cracked or broke at the slightest collision between them. Consequently the boat reached 580 kilograms, including the parts that had been fixed to it – i.e. the hatches, navigation equipment, solar panels, batteries, etc. but not including the provisions, anchors, oars and everything else that could be unloaded from the boat.

Most of the work was carried out by Max and I alone. Quite deliberately, we made the effort to minimise any professional help and on only a few occasions did we need to seek it – when some metal parts needed to be cut by laser or welded as it wasn't worth buying the necessary technology to manufacture just a few elements.

During the build, we had set up two loudspeakers in the garage and we listened to music pretty much all the time we were working. I liked Bulgarian and Brazilian music while Max preferred to listen to rock, rap and the latest mixes from DJs whose names were new to me. With a young man of around 15, sucked into the whirlwind of the everyday – school, homework, computer games, sport, etc., it's difficult to hold a conversation longer than a few words and to get replies, more extensive than "OK", "Yeah" or "No". In the garage working on the boat, however, we had the chance to talk far and wide – to remember stories, to joke around with each other, to make plans. I reminded him of things that happened in his childhood – for example, when he was just three or four years old, he used to play with dinosaurs. He'd collected dozens of small plastic dinosaurs and he could recognise and name them with eyes closed just by touching them. He liked to pretend to be a terrifying dinosaur by lifting his hands above his head with outstretched fingers and uttering throaty roars and I'd pretend to be frightened, which really tickled him. At that time we lived in Brazil where he was born, and we spent every second weekend on the beach. On one occasion, three or four bigger kids gathered around a hole he was digging in the sand and he decided that he could scatter them if he pretended to be a terrifying dinosaur. When he lifted his hands with outstretched fingers and began to give out throaty growls, the bigger kids, instead of getting scared, began to laugh and Max could not believe his eyes. After all, this was something that terrified his father – there was no way these kids wouldn't be scared. He tried again, but the effect was the same. The bigger kids continued to laugh instead of running away. This memory made me reckon up how much we had changed from those moments on the beach, what a road we'd travelled down and what interesting experiences still awaited us both.

Thus, the long laminating process and the whole construction of the boat passed by imperceptibly and very pleasantly. These were countless hours of work, spent in the garage which had become our refuge, a place for sharing time and thoughts.

Some boat building workshops say that to build an ocean rowing boat you need to put in around 16,000 man-hours of work. I think they are exaggerating a little, to justify the exceptionally high prices of their boats, but the necessary man-hours of work was certainly in the thousands. We had time to evaluate different plans for the voyage; which route would be best to take; when would be the opportune time for our launch; what were the risks we had to foresee; and what to do to improve our preparation. We set up lists with countless tasks and crossed them off one by one, but then added more and more; this process felt as if it had no end. When you're having fun and the activities connected to the construction and preparation are constantly changing, you don't think of when everything will finish. We were completely consumed by work on the boat, we were being swallowed by an

MAXIM AND STEFAN IVANOV

unfamiliar world and at the same time we were com-
municating in a way we had never done up until now.

BLACK AND WHITE
6 APRIL 2019, MAX

The work was progressing well. Months of hard
work had passed nevertheless, what remained was
still considerable. We strictly followed the steps, to
be sure we wouldn't miss anything and compromise
the succeeding stages. I insisted that everything met
the highest standards – from both a safety and ap-
pearance point of view. For this reason, I wanted the
final paint job for the boat to look good – it would
feel nicer to live in and look at it for months on end.
We decided therefore, to purchase a compressor and
paint gun to spray paint it, like they do with yachts
and cars. This also required getting astronaut-like
suits to wear and rigging up plastic curtains to avoid
painting ourselves and the interior of the garage the
same colour as the boat. Before starting, we conducted research into what primers and paints to use, how
many coats to apply with the gun, what pressure to
set in the compressor, etc. I felt that although these
activities were not especially exciting, they were still
part of the fun.

My father insisted I take most of the decisions –
from the choice of boat design through to the positioning of hatches and the colour of the paint. I liked
this idea, not because it gave me full control over the
project, but rather it helped me to quickly learn how

to take important key decisions. Together or separately, we researched and evaluated different alternatives, but my father insisted on the final decisions
resting with me and so I came to have a greater influence on the makeup of the boat. As to the colour of
the boat, I hesitated between many variants – from
orange or yellow (which maybe would be more easily seen from a distance if we needed to be rescued)
through black (which I quickly rejected, because the
boat would be burnt up by the sun) to red (like some
sports boats and cars). In the end I decided to paint
the bottom black and the actual boat in classic white.
I decided on white because it looked stylish, and could
be spotted easily from a distance. I used black for the
boat's bottom, in order to coordinate the waterline
with the border between black and white. The idea
was to easily see the rise of the waterline depending
on the weight of the boat.

The painting was my job from beginning to end. I
really had fun with it – from the moment I sprayed
the first coat of black over the keel of the boat and it
looked like an SR 71 Blackbird or some dark submarine. It's good that I started from the bottom. While
laying the first coat, I moved the gun too slowly and
drips of paint formed on the surface which ran down
the hull. By my second attempt though, I got the hang
of the technique and the paint job went on much more
smoothly.

The garage gradually started looking like a real
boat building workshop. Apart from the riveter, jigsaw, drill and compressor, we'd bought more tools
like angle grinders, rotor sanders and others which
saved us incalculable hours of manual work. Every
time we acquired a new tool, my father would say,

"Max, from today you have a new friend, he's called Rotor Sander (or something else). I'm sure you'll get along well." And he'd leave me to work with it for several hours. This happened dozens of times and I'd be constantly finding a new tool and new tasks. I remember how one time I got fed up with new friends (tools) and sometimes when work on the boat exceeded four or five hours a day, it got too much and I resisted. I justified this to myself with the fact that I'd only just turned fifteen, still a young teenager, and I was spending most of my free time building and equipping a boat, and as a result, missing the chance to see my friends. This was truly difficult for me, because I needed to be devoted to this project, while not losing my friends in the process.

It's a relief that neither my father nor I, caused ourselves lasting damage with the power tools – for example, the dangerous angle grinder. I have to admit that the wounds on my father's hands looked many times worse than my injuries. He kept finding ways of cutting or pinching himself. I don't know whether this is because he is clumsy or because I am too careful, but I was sure he'd always have more injuries than me.

Actually, since my childhood I have played the role of 'risk manager' in our family. I remember how, when we were travelling in the car to a lake in the Rhodope mountains and we were following our route on Google Maps, our application sent us off the main road on to a B road and then on to a dirt track which gradually began to climb higher up the mountain and became more broken up and stony. The rains had cut out huge crevices in the track and the rocks became bigger and bigger and at one moment we had to go around rather than over them. My father kept saying, "Nothing to worry about, there's only six kilometres left, just five kilometres...". I advised him to turn around and go back to the asphalt road, so we didn't ruin our family car. In the end I was right, because the dirt track became so impassable that we had to turn back and go around the mountain. The journey finished well, but I think this, and other similar events built trust with my parents – they saw that I paid attention to risks and the consequences of my actions. Thus, gradually, mutual trust was built between us and my parents left me to take care of myself, to make decisions and become more self-sufficient. One of the main reasons my father and I worked so well together, was the contrast in our characters: he liked risk more, which helped us mobilise at important moments, especially in a crisis; while I tended to analyse the situation and take steps to minimise unpleasant or adverse consequences. What emerged was a yin-yang, which perfectly balanced decisions about the boat and the voyage.

Chapter 3

WE LEARN FROM THE VERY BEST
14 DECEMBER 2018, STEFAN

From the very first day of boat construction, Max and I had decided that we would need to find a professional trainer to teach us to row properly. In order to prepare ourselves physically for the challenge that awaited us, we hired a rowing boat by the hour on Pancharevo Lake. Straight away however, we realised that it is not easy to guess when and how to use hands, backs and legs in working the oars. From practising other sports I knew that if you got into the habit of making the wrong movements, firstly, you could suffer serious injuries, secondly, you wouldn't be very effective and thirdly, it would be difficult to change the bad habit already acquired.

I remember how as a youngster, I learnt to swim with the help of my Granddad Kolyo, who couldn't even swim himself. When I decided to swim the Channel, just before my fortieth year, I had to learn from scratch with the help of an unbelievable trainer, Kristian Minkovski, who had trained many of the best swimmers in Bulgaria. Kristian would stand beside the pool during countless sessions, for every one of which he'd plan different exercises, write them down on a little piece of paper that he'd stick to the wet wall of the swimming pool and correct my mistakes methodically and with stoical patience. During these lessons I drank a lot of chlorinated water from the pool, as I was learning to breathe on every third stroke, not on every second – i.e. once to the left side, then to the right side. Kristian introduced us to Rumyana Neykova – many times Olympic and World rowing champion – who for quite some time could not believe that we'd become seriously engaged in the challenge of rowing across the Atlantic.

After several months of messaging and telephone conversations, Rumyana recommended we start preparing ourselves with the help of a rowing trainer, whom she'd introduce us to – Victoria Dimitrova. Both had become world champions in Seville in 2002, where Rumyana won the women's single sculls and Victoria the women's lightweight single sculls. Victoria grabbed the gold, leading at the final from start to finish in front of the ergometer world record holder Lisa Schlenker. The video clip of the final is incredibly exciting and well worth a watch. Victoria was also the youngest rowing competitor in the Bulgarian team in the Sydney Olympics in 2000, where she reached the B-final in double sculls, lightweight category.

We were thrilled to meet Victoria in a café in Sofia and to try to convince her to take us seriously and become our trainer. She did agree, but set us the condition that we complete ten training sessions with her before we all decided what to do further on in our rowing. The first sessions were on the ergometer in the Academic stadium fitness centre. Of course, we began with the basics. Vicky watched over us like a hawk, following our every movement and correcting every mistake. During each session, she'd record videos of how we were rowing and point out to us the differences between correct and incorrect movements. She would constantly adapt and change the targets we were chasing – in settings of load, heart rate, length of rest periods, rowing boat resistance. She introduced specific rowing exercises like waves and rowing machine jumps, back strengthening lifts and other exercises with weights. She closely watched our pre-session warm ups and our cool down afterwards and gave appropriate instructions to make them more effective.

When she decided the moment was right, Vicky got us one by one, into a competitive rowing boat with three other young rowers from the Academic Rowing Club on the Pancharevo Lake for a couple of sessions, just for us to experience what rowing on water was like.

When we eventually finished the construction of our boat, she was the first to step on to it along with us, although at the time she was eight months pregnant with her third child. Vicky did not stop training us and her other trainees, right up until the very day that her son Nikolay was born. After that, she put together a training system on the rowing machine together with strengthening exercises for us to practise at home during the coronavirus pandemic in the last one hundred days before our launch.

During the many hours spent together, she motivated us; she told us educational and funny stories and throughout she was our dream trainer.

When we began training with Vicky, we realised that academic rowing is one of the most arduous sports. It loads and develops muscles throughout the whole body – including those in the legs, back, hands, shoulders and abdominals. During the first few months, we'd finish our sessions really happy, but completely worn out by the enormous energy we'd had to expend. Often we had muscular spasms or pain, especially where our muscles had been trained the least, like in our backs.

A few years earlier, during a family holiday, my daughter Lara and niece Anita Hartland were playing hide-and-seek and got into a deep ditch from which they were unable to climb out of on their own. They called out to me for help. When I lifted them out one by one I heard my back give a loud crack. It turned out I'd fractured a disk in my spine, which forced me to spend several days in bed, attend physiotherapy, and for a long time avoid serious back exercises. As a result of this injury, I was especially careful with the rowing training; I didn't want the pain to return or to get a new injury.

Our plan was to cross the Atlantic Ocean, and for that we had to make over a million strokes. So, the more correct our rowing technique, the more practice we put into preparation, the lower the chances of us getting injured or worse – failing to complete our mission. To be sure of our physical preparation and endurance we began strength training sessions with Yuri Atanasov, a conditioning trainer and one of the few Bulgarian competitors in kettlebell lifting – a sport with kettlebells (weights of 16, 24 or 32 kilogram) with which the competitor has to achieve a maximum number of weight lifts and jerks in ten minutes. Of course, we were not planning to take part in classic kettlebell competitions but with Yuri's help we carried out exercises with weight lifts and squats, with which we trained our bodies for strength and endurance through contortions and other unusual movements. This was really useful because in the ocean, when the boat is being tossed through the waves or the wind is pushing it from one side, symmetrical rowing is not possible like that experienced with a rowing machine or in a classic academic rowing boat; the rower's body is subjected to asymmetrical loads over the duration of many hours.

Physical preparation was just one of the challenges. The expedition we'd decided to undertake was a whole new world for us; one which demanded education, planning, decision making and so much more. That's what made it so immense and so incredibly exciting.

Chapter 4

YES! TO LIFE!
MARCH 2019, MAX

Almost all ocean rowers choose a charitable cause to which to dedicate their voyage. This way they direct society's attention to a beneficial and important idea and their voyage does not remain a sole end in itself. I knew that when there was an additional motivation I'd be even more purposeful and determined to succeed. We found out that ocean rowing expeditions have helped in raising funds for hospitals, orphanages, victims of disasters, and all kinds of health, ecological and social causes. All these causes were meaningful and the results achieved, rendered an additional worth to the physical and psychological efforts of the rowers during their expedition.

My family and I discussed many worthy causes and campaigns. In the end it came down to three: 1) to raise funds to build wells in distant parts of Africa, where people have to walk many kilometres every day to fetch water to their homes; 2) to contribute to the dredging of mud deposits in Pancharevo Lake. This was the only place in the close vicinity of Sofia, where rowing training could take place, and which sadly is becoming blocked with sediment. This not only caused problems for the development of amateur rowing but also hampered the competitive rowers, who were unable to train on the classic two-kilometre competition course but instead had to turn around every one kilometre. This is a similar problem to training for a swimming race in a 25-metre pool, when you ought to be training in a 50-metre pool; 3) to support the Yes! To life! campaign of the Ministry of Health. Its aim is to raise public awareness about organ donation and to help more people make an informed decision to become donors after death.

The attention of the whole family was captured by this campaign and we embraced the idea wholeheartedly. According to the Ministry of Health, over 1150 people in Bulgaria were awaiting the transplant of a vital organ, and up until now barely fifty transplants are performed each year. These statistics suggested that those in need would have to wait for a life-saving organ for ten years on average, which in reality meant that many of them would not be able to await it. This seemed absurd and unacceptable to me and I wanted to do what I could to contribute to the cause.

All these people are waiting for a second chance for life, which is possible only through an organ transplant. In 2019, out of the 28 member states of the EU, our country was last in the number of transplants per million inhabitants. Because of the insufficient number of donors and the frequent refusal of their relatives to donate the organs of the deceased, the Ministry of Health started the national campaign for support of donorship and transplantation with the slogan Yes! To life!

In Spain, which for 28 years has been the world leader in transplantations, in 2019 the number of deceased donors was 49 per million inhabitants. On average in Europe this number is 17, but in Bulgaria it is just 2.

My father insisted I choose the cause which we will support, and with no hesitation I decided on Yes! To life!. Later I understood this would have been his first choice as well. We'd get involved in motivating more people to take the decision to become organ donors after their death and to share their wishes with their family. In Bulgaria those closest to the deceased have the last word. The law on the transplantation of organs, tissues and cells states that "the removal of organs from a deceased person can take place when (…) an advance warning of their forthcoming removal has been made, and no refusal has been lodged in a reasonably short period by their: a) spouse or parent; b) child; c) brother or sister". However, as the law does not mention presumed consent, in the absence of refusal, as it does in other places (like England, etc.), doctors currently seek an explicit agreement from those closest to the deceased. In the event of refusal, the organs of the deceased are not used for transplant. The family often cannot take such a decision, if they are not aware in advance of the will of the deceased.

For us this was an exceptionally noble cause, because it came down to the saving of human lives, and miraculously without anyone being hurt, as the organs of the deceased are not necessary to them or to their family. Sadly in many cases these organs go to feed worms or are cremated; these are countless missed chances to save lives. I imagined myself not in the position of the donor or their family, but in that of the person in need. Thus it became painfully clear to me how critical the situation in Bulgaria was, and therefore the huge significance of this campaign.

We got in touch with the Ministry of Health and got their agreement to join in the promotion of the Yes! To life! campaign. We explained to them that our expedition would probably attract some media attention, giving us the chance to talk about the campaign and thus reaching a wider audience.

Until this moment, we had not made any mention of the building of the boat and our plans to cross the ocean to anyone outside our circle of close relatives and friends. We had not published any information about the expedition we were planning on our social media profiles. We had left this part of the project on the back burner and we really hadn't got to it, because we were not seeking popularity. But once we had decided to get involved in the campaign, things changed. We needed to reach more followers and to promote more conversations on the subject of donorship. Ahead of us a new action front would be added to our voyage plans. I began to understand that what we were engaged in was taking on even more significance, our responsibility was also increasing, and our project was leaving the confines of our tight circle and was turning into a challenge of social worth. We were about to find out whether our expedition would change not only us, but society's opinion on such an important subject as organ donorship.

Chapter 5

MEETINGS WITH OCEAN ROWERS
APRIL 2019 - FEBRUARY 2020, STEFAN

For a long time we researched and gathered recommendations for what equipment to buy and install on the boat. In December 2019, I even travelled to San Sebastián de la Gomera in the Canary Islands before the start of the yearly ocean rowing race, the Talisker Whisky Atlantic Challenge, to look over the 35 boats taking part that year and to talk to the ocean rowers about equipment, food, preparation and everything which would be useful during the voyage. It was thrilling to hear stories of successful and unsuccessful voyages, as well as of the preparations of these brave men and women for this present voyage. They readily told me of the adversities and their plans, and I made the effort to assimilate important lessons and grew ever more excited by what lay ahead of us. Many of their recommendations were repeated, which was encouraging.

In the end I put together a list of essential equipment and this included:

Navigational equipment:

- Chartplotter Raymarine eS75 with Raymarine RS150 GPS. This is a device with a big screen, on which you see a detailed map of the voyage region, including coastline, rocks, harbours, fairways, buoys, depths and all other details. It measures and shows:

  – COG (Course Over Ground) – the true direction in which the boat is travelling (e.g. 240 degrees). This is really useful information as the course of the boat through most of its voyage differs from the direction of the prow, because the wind and currents are almost constantly driving it sideways.

  – SOG (Speed Over Ground) – the combined result of our rowing efforts and the effects of the winds, currents, waves and barnacles stuck to the boat's hull, etc. At times, it prompts us that it is time we scraped the hull, but more often it reminds us to row faster.

  – DTW (Distance To Waypoint) – on the chart we could mark up various waypoints which we wanted to row to, for example, the final destination, an island or the next point where we'd change course, and this would immediately show the straight line distance to it.

  – BTW (Bearing To Waypoint) – shows what course we have to keep to reach the next waypoint.

- Raymarine AIS700 (Automatic Identification System) – this is a device which communicates with satellites and marks out on the chartplotter our exact position, as well as those of seagoing vessels around us, their direction and speed of travel. When the device calculates there is a danger of our boat colliding with another vessel, with the shore, with a buoy, or with some other object, it begins to sound a loud alarm.

- Additional small screen Raymarine i70s, which draws information from the chartplotter about the latitude and longitude of our position, Course Over Ground, Speed Over Ground, the distance and course to the next waypoint, etc. We installed it at the feet of the rower, so that while he rows, he can navigate the boat on his own even at night time.
- Autopilot Raymarine ST2000 – a device with a compass and a mechanical arm which moves the tiller to starboard or portside, so that the boat's prow is continuously aimed in the selected direction.
- Raymarine p70s controller, with which the rower can control the autopilot.
- Several hand-held compasses and a big one, Polare Riviera, with a light which we also installed at the rower's feet to help him navigate the boat.

Communication equipment:
- Satellite telephone Iridium 9575 which works like a normal mobile phone but not through cell towers on the ground, but through satellites, orbiting the earth. Because of this you occasionally get sound delays and breakup of conversation especially when it's very cloudy or rainy.
- Satellite hotspot Iridium GO!, which we arc to use in conjunction with a smart telephone for sending and receiving emails, photos and SMSs,

as well as downloading meteorological forecasts and enabling conversations.

- Satellite device YB3 with a tracker through which our location, direction and speed will appear every few hours on the website https:my.yb.tl/neverest, so that our navigators, family and friends can follow in real time where we are, and how we are getting on. Through this device we can send and receive short emails, so as to have a two way contact with our land based team, in case both our Iridium devices stop working.
- Built-in VHF radio Ray53 through which to communicate with ships and ports, located no further than a score of nautical miles away.
- Hand-held very high frequency radio Enel HC 644 VHF, to use if the built-in radio or the electrical system powering it stop working.
- EPIRB (Emergency Position Indicating Radio Beacon) ACR GlobalFix Pro 406 MHz with a red button to push in the event of an emergency. The device sends a coded message via the satellites to the nearest Rescue Coordination Centre, to enable it to organise a rescue. The centre will connect with ships close to the distressed vessel and coordinate which of them will attend the rescue. According to marine law, ships are duty bound to help except when they have someone seriously ill on board or they are carrying goods that can quickly spoil. If they don't respond they can be heavily sanctioned. The Rescue Coordination Centre can even include aeroplanes or helicopters in the rescue if this is necessary

or possible depending on the location of the emergency.

- Two PLB (Personal Locator Beacon) Ocean Signal rescueME devices, each the size of half a fist, which we fastened to our belts. Along with one of them, each of us used rope to tie himself to the boat when going out on deck. It performs the same function as the EPIRB.

With all these devices on board our boat began to resemble a space capsule. For boys like us it was absolutely fascinating to research and test these devices. The team of Shiptechnics in Varna which equips yachts and ships with technology, helped us not only in the selection of some of the devices, but with their testing and configuration and the exchange of those that turned out to be faulty. The AIS, for example, resolutely refused to work when the boat was in front of our garage in Sofia, but when we sent it twice to Varna, it worked perfectly there. In the end they discovered that according to its factory settings the AIS switched itself off when it was located over 500 metres above sea level, perhaps so it couldn't be used for terrorist purposes in rockets or airplanes. Just in case, however, they installed on loan a second AIS free of charge, so we wouldn't be invisible to bigger ships.

EVERY DETAIL IS IMPORTANT
15 MAY 2019, MAX

Time was passing and the work of constructing and equipping our boat was progressing. The process engaged us. We discussed and planned several steps ahead. Alongside the work in the garage, we researched what we were going to need on the voyage. Now that the boat had taken on an almost completed look, painted and looking like a real marine beauty, the time came to install all kinds of requisites and accessories. It was fun to look at photos and videos of ocean rowing boats, to pore over online catalogues for boat parts and to pay many visits to several specialised shops in Sofia. We wanted to select better quality and sturdier elements to minimise the risks of breakdown in the middle of the ocean, where it is impossible to receive spare part deliveries! In spite of taking an active part in this process, I somehow could not believe that we would really need the equipment we were buying. The idea of the crossing, however clear it was, still seemed abstract and unreal to me.

We decided to order the oars from Australia – from Crocker Oars, a company, which was founded more than 50 years ago, whose oars were used by the majority of medallists in the Olympic and international rowing championships. For several years now Crocker Oars have produced reinforced oars, adapted especially for ocean rowing. We got in touch with Darren Crocker – the son of the company's founder, who explained to us how they manufacture the oars, how we should use them and care for them and even how to glue them if we accidentally manage to break them in the ocean. We ordered two pairs of oars and a month later they arrived in Sofia.

As we did not know what hatches, oarlocks, sliding seats, footplates, drogue anchor and other parts and accessories would be most suitable, we decided to buy them from Rannoch Adventure – an English company which, in the last several years, has built most of the world's ocean rowing boats. Its founder, Charley Pitcher, and some of his colleagues who had rowed the oceans several times, responded to our questions and sold us some of the products which they used in the construction and equipping of their boats. They even gave us the electrical system plans, which they used for the connection of the devices, batteries and solar panels on the boat and recommended navigational devices and models.

We put together the sliding seat ourselves, using the two rails which Rannoch Adventure supplied us. Over these rails were positioned axles with wheels attached just like those on ordinary large rollerblades. We managed to work up a spare seat and we bought three sets of wheels and bearings for them, because on the ocean it's sensible to have spare parts for all the boat's components, including those you think you won't need. We thought the bearings might rust from the continual contact with salt water. Therefore, we thoroughly questioned Kalin Staykov – a Bulgarian inline downhill rollerblading contestant, about which were the toughest wheels and the best water-resistant bearings and took those he recommended, in order to minimise the resistance in the movement of the sliding seat over the deck of the boat and the likelihood of the bearings rusting too quickly.

After we had installed the oarlocks for the oars, the sliding seat and the footplates, we sought help from Svilen Neykov – our trainer Victoria's rowing trainer who had prepared many of the best Bulgarian rowers and who in her view was the greatest authority in Bulgaria on rowing and rigging competitive boats. We asked him to help us to make a precise setting for the positions of the seat and the oars, so as to increase the efficiency of our rowing and to reduce the potential for sustaining injuries from the endless rowing action. Luckily, Svilen and his wife Rumyana Neykova responded with joy to our request, and not only helped us with this precise setting, but shared with us some useful advice about rowing and about nutrition for the voyage. Before starting out Rumyana loaned us a third pair of oars, just in case.

DIRECTION OF TRAVEL
29 JULY 2019, STEFAN

The rudder is the flat blade that's fastened at the stern or under the hull of the boat which manages the direction of its travel.

In our case we had to employ our ingenuity to decide exactly what rudder to use and how to fasten it simultaneously to the stern of the boat and to the autopilot which would keep the prow pointed in a given direction. We found out that if we want to reduce the resistance of the rudder in the water to a minimum, it has to have a given NACA profile so it is more streamlined. On the other hand, we wanted to be able to lift and drop it easily while we were training in shallower waters, so as not to break it by hitting the bottom. We were delighted when we discovered the small Latvian firm, Dotan, which manufactures rudders of various sizes that could be lifted and dropped into the water in just one up-and-down movement of the tiller. The blades of their rudders were manufactured from fibreglass like the hull of our boat, they had very well streamlined NACA profiles and they could be fastened to the boat's stern with two pintles mounted on a box from composite material similar to plastic, which connected the rudder blade to the tiller.

For a significant time we researched and deliberated before finally choosing the right size of rudder, too small and it wouldn't be effective in holding a specific course; too big and it would create too much resistance in the water. We chose a model, which when fastened to our boat's stern, reached 57 centimetres below the waterline and had a wetted area of 0.19 square metres, which relative to the wetted area of the boat of 1.5 square metres made up 13%. Nowhere did we find recommendations for these proportions specifically regarding rowing boats, which travel a lot more slowly than yachts and ships, so we had to work on a trial and error basis.

To fasten the rudder box to the autopilot, we manufactured a metal frame out of profiles of stainless steel and bolts. We screwed it with three big bolts to the rudder box, and attached a fourth bolt sticking up, to which we threaded the autopilot arm, so that when it moved back and forth, the rudder turned left and right. We then found an arc welder who welded the different components together to make this metal frame even stronger.

After we had bought and installed the rudder and autopilot, the Dutch ocean rower, Marcel Ates got in touch. He had seen a photo of our boat and wanted to tell us that in his opinion the rudder was too small. Marcel thought that when the stern of the boat was lifted by the waves, a large part of the rudder would leave the water and this could hamper navigation and lead to the autopilot overheating. We thought over what he had to say and manufactured two plates of stainless steel with which we could lower the rudder blade 22 centimetres deeper in the water. We decided to set out without installing them in advance, so as not to increase rudder resistance, but we'd be ready to install them if we encountered problems with navigating the boat or the autopilot overheating. Just in case we took and assembled two complete rudder sets, including two rudder blades, two boxes and two frames. The rudder is an exceptionally important part of the boat and we didn't want to take any risk of remaining without one!

Chapter 6

THE NORTH ATLANTIC ROUTE
JULY 2019, MAX

While we were building the boat, we discussed different ocean routes which we could take. Rowing boats had crossed almost all oceans, but most of them went from Europe (mostly from the Canary Islands) to the Caribbean Islands. We learnt that since 1997, the biggest ocean rowing race has been taking place annually, in which 20 to 30 boats competed from San Sebastián de la Gomera, in the Canary Islands to Antigua, one of the Caribbean Islands, crossing about 2550 nautical miles (4700 kilometres).

As much as we admired the rowing competitors, we preferred to undertake a rowing trip on our own rather than take part in this competition. Firstly, because we dreamed of feeling like ocean explorers and adventurers, learning more about our physical and psychological states everyday while also discovering the extraordinary world of the ocean. We thought that if we were part of a race or if there was a rescue boat close to us, the experience would not be the same and we wouldn't have achieved it 'on our own'. Secondly, the race was always staged in the December to February period, when on this route the Trade Winds blow mostly at your tail, however, this period of time was when I had to be in school and as I was entering 11th grade, taking exams and preparing for university, this was too important a time to miss. Thirdly, if we set out before 10th of August 2020 and crossed the Atlantic successfully, I'd become the youngest ocean rower in the world!

We found out that in the period from June to September, which would coincide with my summer holiday, only a handful of boats succeeded in crossing the North Atlantic – from Canada or the US to Europe. More precisely, 29 out of 74 boats managed it.

The North Atlantic route from Newfoundland, Canada to the Isles of Scilly in the UK seemed an option. It was shorter – about 1820 nautical miles (3370 kilometres) and the record for its crossing of 38 days, 6 hours and 49 minutes was established by a solo oarsman, the American Bryce Carlson. We thought we had a chance to beat his record, and perhaps even the overall record for crossing the Atlantic which was held by the quartet of rowers, the Four Oarsmen, who'd crossed the longer southern route in the winter, from the Canaries to the Caribbean Islands in 29 days, 13 hours and 34 minutes.

We discovered that on the North Atlantic route we'd have to contend with storms and cold – average air and water temperatures close to Newfoundland were about 4 degrees Celsius and the water temperature around the UK did not get higher than 18 degrees Celsius. In order to learn firsthand what to expect on this route, we got in touch with two ocean rowers who'd crossed it successfully – Bryce Carlson and Mylène Paquette.

I was surprised that Bryce Carlson, a record holder for this route, agreed to answer our questions, bearing in mind that eventually we might take his record. Bryce was a teacher and ultramarathon competitor – he had run about 5000 kilometres from the East to the West coasts of America. He gave us valuable information about food which he'd eaten on his voyage, about the prevailing winds and currents and believe it or not (for me it was hard to believe) he sent us a full list of everything which he had taken with him, including underpants and socks, knives, toothbrushes, telephones, books, cups and plates, etc. He even wrote down the makes of all the devices he'd selected – communications, navigation and others. This is what you call a good sportsman.

As for the Canadian, Mylène Paquette, who had rowed solo the distance of 2700 nautical miles (5000 kilometres) from Halifax, Nova Scotia to Lorient, France in 128 days and 22 hours, she became our guardian angel. Before we started out she spent many hours on the telephone and through email with us and my mother, giving us invaluable advice. She told us how quite a few ocean rowers had to abort their voyages because they'd been scalded by boiling water from their gas cookers, when their boats were being tossed around by the ocean waves. She sent us photos of the apparatus she'd employed to keep her gas cooker vertical. It looked like a gyroscope and was made up of three rings, joined together in several places. Of course, my father and I really enjoyed manufacturing such an apparatus from strips of stainless steel and coming up with a way of fastening and unfastening it to the outside wall of the cabin. It worked wonderfully during the voyage.

It was from Mylène that we first heard about the Jordan series drogue, which was made up of a long rope, on which, at every few feet, a small cone was attached with its bottom cut out. Its function is to be fastened to the stern when the wind is too strong and/or the waves are too high, to stop the boat from capsizing. We already had a para anchor, the kind that all ocean rowing boats used, but this is usually tied to the prow in order to hold it as stationary as possible, with respect to the water. The Jordan series drogue is more useful when you have a strong tailwind, as it allows the boat to move over the water, while at the same time preventing it from capsizing. We discovered a small firm in America called Ace Sailmakers, which was authorised to produce this kind of anchor by its inventor, Don Jordan. We ordered 50 cones, after which we knotted them into the rope with our own hands, following instructions from Dave from Ace Sailmakers. Given that neither he nor my father and I knew the right number of cones to use for our rowing boat, we decided to divide them into two groups: first we knotted 30 cones, then we left 10 metres of rope and knotted the remaining 20 – so we could easily cast into the water either 30 or 50 cones and experiment. If necessary we could order still more, or we could remove some of the ones we'd already knotted. At one end of the rope we created a bridle which served to fix the anchor to the stern, and at the other end we put a weight of stainless steel chain – just as Dave had advised us. As it happened, on the voyage we realised that the 50 cone drogue did a wonderful job for the size of our boat – when we cast the drogue from the stern, the prow would turn in the wind's direction and the boat would move in this direction at a half to one knot. Nikolay Djambazov had used for decades a similar drogue anchor with knots instead of cones, which he'd tied to his yacht's stern during storms.

Mylène also shared with us the lists of medicines she'd taken, told us about the food she'd eaten, the storms she'd encountered, etc. It was very invigorating and motivating to listen to how she'd coped with the North Atlantic. Her experiences gave me courage and inspired me with confidence in my own abilities. I told myself that if she could cope completely on her own, the pair of us had a chance to do it. Apart from that, I was learning more and more from conversations with ocean rowers and more about the actual ocean crossing which reduced my anxiety and rid me of the feeling that our undertaking was unachievable. Thus in the end, our resolve hardened to try the North Atlantic route – from Newfoundland to the Isles of Scilly.

TO FIND ONE'S OWN EVEREST
AUGUST 2019, MAX

By now you will surely have guessed that the honour of naming the boat fell to me. Following a seafaring tradition, many boat owners christen them with the name of their beloved woman. My father joked that at long last he'd find out the name of my girlfriend. To be honest, we had some ideas for a name, but none satisfied us completely. We sought different variants, threw out ideas and commented on them. We wanted the name to have some symbolism, to have some positive charge. In the end we decided on the name NEVEREST, in which we weaved the English words NEVER, REST and EVEREST, so it would carry the motto: *Never rest until you reach your Everest.*

When I was training karate in the Karate Club Olymp, Sensei Malin Malinov – the only Bulgarian sixth Dan black belt in Goju Ryu Karate, often used to say: "You'll rest in the grave. While you're alive you can only get a time-out." I really loved Karate training and Sensei Malin Malinov and his son, Sensei Stefan Malinov – third Dan black belt in Goju Ryu Karate, were fantastic trainers and important teachers in my life.

Unfortunately however, it became just impossible to cram studying, sleeping, eating, working on the boat, intensive rowing training and everything else into a 24 hour programme so I had to put Karate on hold. I didn't want to abandon it, but I knew I had to for a while, so that I could concentrate on the task which I had undertaken. That is why I wanted the symbolism and motto of our boat to remind me of the road I'd walked down and the things that I had to give up. I wanted the name to remind me of my Everest, all the difficulties and hard work in climbing my personal peak. NEVEREST evoked associations within me of qualities like endurance, resolve and persistence. Fortunately, everyone in the family really liked this name and approved of my choice.

LET THERE BE LIGHT
AUGUST 2019 - FEBRUARY 2020, STEFAN

In order to provide electricity for all the appliances on board, we had to install solar panels and rechargeable batteries. I sought out my fellow pupil from the Sofia English Language School – Emil Kiossev, who for many years had been working on the manufacture of solar panels as well as the installation of all kinds of electrical systems. He gladly raced in to help with the specifications and installation of the boat's electrical system.

Up to this point in time, almost all ocean rowing boats were equipped with lead-acid batteries, which Phil – our boat's designer, had also advised us to use. However, the first piece of advice that Emo enthusiastically and persuasively gave us, was to forget such out of date things and to get ourselves some lithium-ion rechargeable batteries because they were almost half the weight, could be charged more quickly and frequently, there was no problem for them to be discharged at down to 20% instead of 50% of their capacity and they had built-in BMSs (Battery Management Systems). With Emo's help we chose and installed two lithium-ion batteries (Victron Lithium SuperPack – 12.8V/100Ah and 12.8V/60Ah), charge controllers (Victron SmartSolar MPPT 75/15) and battery monitors (Victron BMV 700), as well as four Ekoflex flexible solar panels with a maximum combined power of 310 watts. We could follow, through the Victron application on our phones, exactly how many watts in real time were generated by each panel, how many watt-hours of electrical energy were produced during the past several days, etc. At any point in time, we could check to what percentage they'd been charged, how many hours remained until their discharge at the same rate of power consumption, etc. on the battery monitors.

We had to festoon the whole boat with cables. For this purpose, we brought in pipes and waterproofed their passage between different storage holds and the cabin. We created two independent electrical circuits, so that our electrical appliances could be fed by each of the rechargeable batteries separately or both together. We installed a separate controller for each solar panel, so that every component of the electrical system could be switched off if it was damaged and the system would continue to work without it. We installed the chartplotter, the AIS, built-in radio station, battery monitors, stereo and keys for switching each appliance on and off in waterproof boxes in the cabin, so that we could protect them as much as possible from damage in case they got wet or flooded. We also put the rechargeable batteries and their charging controllers into separate waterproof boxes in the big bow and aft storage compartments and we glued the boxes to the bottom of the boat, so they would not move and fall on to the ceilings of these compartments in the event of the boat rocking or even capsizing.

We also bought a small solar panel with an inbuilt battery which would be completely independent of the boat's electrical system. We could use this to at least charge up the satellite phone and the YB3 tracker if the main electrical system went out of action. For the same reason we ordered a manual dynamo from China, but ultimately it failed to arrive before we set out on our voyage.

To the electrical system, we connected a Schenker Zen 30 watermaker – an apparatus with a compressor and lots of filters which desalinises the seawater and makes it potable. When we were installing it in the garage, the compressor cut out from time to time, so we had to spend a significant number of hours on the phone with the manufacturer in Italy to buy a refractometer – a device for measuring the salt content of the water, which we'd brought in bottles from the Aegean Sea in order to perform our various tests. One of the possible reasons for the cutting out, was that the temperature in the garage was too low – about 15 degrees Celsius, which led to the increase of pressure in the system over 8 atmospheres instead of the expected 6-7. Since we intended to cross the North Atlantic where the temperatures of water and air were expected to fall below 4 degrees Celsius, we calibrated the system for the purpose. In the end, it turned out that the cutting out of the compressor was down to the fact that a vicious circle had been created: each time the water passed through the filters, the clean, drinkable water was taken out through a narrow hose to a small barrel and the rest, which was actually a larger quantity, we simply put back into the big barrel, into which we'd poured the original bottles of salt water. Thus the salt content of the water in the big barrel was continually increasing which increased the pressure in the system as that water passed through the filters. After we broke this vicious circle, everything normalised. We knew that many ocean rowers had encountered problems with their watermakers, so we decided to take a lot of spare parts for ours – including a reserve compressor, multiway switch, hoses, etc.

We also took a manual watermaker Katadyn 35 Survivor – in case we had problems with the electric watermaker or with the electrical system. It worked on the same principle of sieving sea water through filters but instead of using a compressor, one had to manually pump with a long handle to create the necessary pressure.

THE END OF ONE THING IS THE BEGINNING OF ANOTHER
AUGUST 2019 - MAY 2020, STEFAN

If you think that everything finished with the painting of the boat, you'd be very much mistaken. I also thought that once Max had applied three coats of primer and two-component polyurethane paint with the spray gun and compressor, we'd consider the process of working on the boat's body as completed. We had more to learn at this point. We shared the stages through which we had passed with the manufacturers at SEA LINE and they advised us to take a few more steps to completely finish the process. We had to sand down the last coat of paint with a very fine sandpaper either by hand or with a vibro-sander and then clean the surface once more by hand with a micro-fibre cloth soaked with a SEA LINE S3 Finish Cleaner. Further actions followed such as:

- Application of a polishing paste SEA LINE Soft Cut and Gloss with a polishing machine using a lamb's wool pad.
- Application of another polishing paste SEA LINE Extra Shine Hologram Remover with a polishing machine again using lamb's wool pad.
- Application of anti-fouling coating on the boat's hull, to prevent or at least reduce marine life attaching to it. After significant research we decided on McLube Antifoul Alternative Speed Polish, because we discovered that in recent years this coating has been used by most competitors in the Olympic yacht races and in the big yachting regattas. In contrast to the usual antifoul paints which contain toxic components for marine life, this alternative product contains citrus elements which carry out the same function, even though not fully effectively.

After all this, it fell to us to apply a non-slip covering over the boat deck. We'd already sensed how slippery it could be, especially when it was wet. We chose to apply KiwiGrip Non-skid Coating on the places we reckoned to step on the most on deck and finally we were finished with the painting and polishing.

With these final strokes it was as if the construction of NEVEREST was over. It could be said that it happened quite quickly or there again very slowly. I could not decide whether it was a joyful or sad moment. Personally I prefer to live in the present, to feel with my senses the moment in which I find myself. I have to admit that while we were constructing the boat, I hadn't thought of the moment when it would be ready and everything would finish and how that would make me feel. However, I'm not one to be distracted by nostalgia for all the pleasant moments when we succeeded in solving some engineering head-scratcher, achieving a beautiful shape in some element of the boat or installing some interesting device on board. When a monumental effort comes to an end, that warm feeling of satisfaction pours out in my soul – as they say in Bulgarian like drops of honey on the heart.

Chapter 7

THE CHILDHOOD DREAM TO BECOME A CAPTAIN
SUMMER 2019, MAX

When my father was around my age – a teenager – he dreamed of being the captain of a big ship. Instead of rock band posters, his bedroom walls were covered with pictures of tankers, container-ships, chemical-cargo boats and other kinds of ships.

During the 1980s, when Bulgaria was in the Communist bloc and it was almost impossible for anyone to travel around the world, not only did you need a visa to visit other countries, but also special permission to leave Bulgaria. Through the eyes of my father, sailors were among the lucky ones who could travel round the world with no limitations and captains were experienced and brave men, who bore responsibility for everything happening on board their ships. Sadly in his teenage years my father developed short-sightedness and concluded that he would be unlikely to pass the captaincy exam and even if he did, the concern of potentially breaking or losing his glasses in a sea storm, putting the whole crew at risk, troubled his thoughts.

Today it's not a problem to sign up for and complete a course as skipper of a sea going vessel up to 40 BT (Brute tonnage), even if you're short-sighted. I am also short-sighted and I had been wearing glasses for two years, but this didn't get in the way of taking a skipper's course (Note: I could not get a skipper's certificate, because I wasn't 18 years old).

On the recommendation of Nikolay Djambazov we contacted Karelia Sailing School in Sofia, and the instructors, Stefan Karamanliev and Peter Stoimenov were kind enough to accept us both on the skipper's course, though I was just a listener during the theoretical part and couldn't actually take the exam. My father however passed the exam, taken at the Executive Agency, Maritime Administration correctly answering 59 out of a total of 60 questions and thus received his skipper's certificate entitling him to take command of a seagoing vessel of up to 40 BT. The instructors, Stefan and Peter, taught us many useful things – including how to safely pass another sea vessel, how to identify the different buoys and other warning signs on the sea or on the coastline, how to tie sailors' and other knots, and many other useful things. They were rightly annoyed however, that some of the questions in the skipper's exam included unimportant information which the course students had to learn by heart, for example, the definition of a jibboom – an additional wooden mast which extends from the bowsprit on a sailing vessel!

It was not compulsory, but we decided that it would also be useful if we undertook a VHF (very high frequency) radio operator's course. We contacted the Sailing BG School, which is a centre in Bulgaria licensed by the RYA (Royal Yachting Association) in the United Kingdom. The instructor, Tanya Djachkova and her husband Vencislav Dobrinov were the owners of the school, and sailors who had crossed seas and oceans themselves. When they heard about our planned adventure, they not only offered us the radio course for free, but gave us some books and other teaching aids, related to sea travel. Before setting out on the expedition they regularly phoned us to ask us whether we had thought of this or that, whether we had everything necessary, were we clear about the details which could prove important during the voyage, etc. They also introduced us to their friend, Kolio Bozakov (Kole Kole) who organised ocean fishing trips.

Kole was a very busy man, but he found time to meet my father at a fishing tackle shop a few hours before we departed, in order to select lines, hooks and lures which he thought we'd find useful in the ocean and explained how to use them. He showed him how to fillet a big fish if we catch one so we can eat it raw, a la sashimi. I adore salmon sashimi as well as all kinds of sushi, so much so that every week I begged my mother to prepare it at home. She's now made it so many times that she makes it better than all the sushi restaurants in Sofia that we've been to. She likes experimenting with food and has the confidence to prepare all kinds of new dishes. Of course, I like to try new dishes too, believing in the English proverb: 'Variety is the spice of life'.

THE LAUNCH OF NEVEREST
16 AUGUST 2019, MAX

At last the moment came to try out the boat on Pancharevo Lake. I couldn't quite believe we had made it this far. Stefan Karamanliev had told us anecdotally about an old gentleman who had, like us, decided to build a boat in his garage and sail it to Canada to visit his daughter. He had also undertaken the skipper course, however Stefan felt awkward teaching him because he worried that the gentleman was too old and wouldn't manage it. By teaching him on the course, Stefan felt complicit in this risky undertaking. He hoped that when the gentleman went for a medical check-up, they'd turn him down for this or that reason. After that, he hoped that they'd fail him in the exam at Maritime Administration, but he passed it, answering more questions correctly than any of his fellow students – he clearly was strongly motivated to achieve his dream. So in the end, this man finished building his boat (out of metal) and took it to Pancharevo Lake to test it out. Clearly a lot of people had heard about this undertaking and there gathered quite a crowd of curious onlookers, including journalists. However, when the boat was launched into the water, it almost immediately sank! I wasn't sure if this story was true, or Stefan was simply trying to put us off going through with our plan, but I was slightly worried whether NEVEREST would hold up when we launched it into water.

Before taking the boat to Pancharevo, we'd asked one of the trainers at the rowing base there whether we could use the lake ramp from which most boats were launched as well as the crane beside it, with which we could carry out a test for capsizing. This was an important test, to be sure that if in the ocean the boat was turned upside down by the waves, it would right itself.

We were amateurs and although we'd applied all our knowledge and energies into the construction of NEVEREST, within us there still lurked a doubt as to whether the boat was fit for an ocean voyage. The experienced Bulgarian yachtsman Captain Nikolay Djambazov had recommended that we load the boat to the maximum, similar to how the boat would be loaded on our ocean voyage and to carry out several tests – with a rower or weights in his position in the cabin and on the deck. Such a capsizing test can be carried out quite easily – a rope is tied to the two cleats on one side of the boat, it's passed under the boat and is tied on the other side to a crane's hook. When the crane pulls the rope the boat turns turtle. The trainer said that he would assist us, but when the next day we arrived with the boat, he began backing out of the agreement.

The honour of the first oar-strokes in NEVEREST fell to me. I got into the boat, my father manoeuvred the trailer down the ramp and began to turn the handle of the winch which was tied to the boat's prow. The boat gradually began to pull away from the trailer until in the end it was launched free on the water. Like a white swan, it sat graciously in the water. Truth be told, we were not too worried that it would sink at its first dip, we wondered more about the possibility it might lean to one side or rock too much, or whether it would have difficulty actually moving through the water. We had decided not to invite relatives and friends to NEVEREST's first launch as it was in the middle of the coronavirus pandemic and we didn't want to take any unnecessary risks. In fact, we hadn't even brought a bottle of champagne to break on the boat's prow! Fortunately, it turned out that NEVEREST was born for the water and without having a serious basis for comparison, it seemed to me to be both a stable and easily manoeuvrable boat. I pulled several strokes with the oars, expecting it to be heavy and difficult to manoeuvre, but in reality it required no great exertion to distance myself from the shore and then to steer it smoothly close to the wharf where my father met me. Dipping the oars, I felt how smoothly the boat cut through the water and that I had control over it. I bristled with joy and satisfaction as I realised that the thousands of hours in the garage had been utterly worth it and an enormous smile spread across my face. Of course, the calm Pancharevo Lake was a long way from our target, but I thought the first launch of the boat had gone remarkably well.

THE OFFICIAL REGISTRATION OF NEVEREST
AUGUST 2019, STEFAN

In order to row the boat on different seas and oceans and to transport it through border posts, we had to register it. Ordinance No. 68 of the Maritime Administration agency designates five alternative regions for voyages and all seafaring vessels must be registered to one of them:

– *Region I – navigation on inner seaways and the territorial waters of the Republic of Bulgaria and in the seas and oceans which is subdivided into: sub-region I-B up to 5 nautical miles from the coast and sub-region I-C up to 12 nautical miles from the coast;*

– *Region II – navigation up to 20 nautical miles from the coast;*

– *Region III – navigation up to 60 nautical miles from the coast;*

– *Region IV – navigation up to 200 nautical miles from the coast;*

– *Region V – unlimited region for navigation.*

We, of course, needed permission for Region V, but as you can imagine, because the Maritime Administration agency in Bulgaria had not heard of ocean rowing boats, they didn't accept a single word about this region. Ordinance No. 68 listed all the requirements for seagoing vessels related to their engines, hulls, construction, navigational equipment, signalling and rescue equipment, firefighting equipment, radio appliances, medical supplies, etc. without distinguishing between ships, yachts and rowing boats.

We had to therefore, additionally purchase many more items such as more rescue vests, red parachute rockets and hand-held flares, floating smoke flares, thermo-suits, a waterproof electric torch, a horn for sound signals, etc. There were only two things we didn't take with us – a radar and a floating platform, because they were too big and wouldn't fit on the boat. As we had signalling flares and rockets, as well as the gas cooker on which we'd boil water, on board, we also bought two fire extinguishers – one we fastened to the wall of the cabin, and the other in the big aft hold. On the wall of the cabin we put a small box in which we kept a fire blanket.

The Maritime Administration agency wanted to see the calculations of the boat's designer/engineer regarding the boat's stability subject to tilting, so Phil Morrison sent us information generated from the software with which he'd designed the boat (see figure 2).

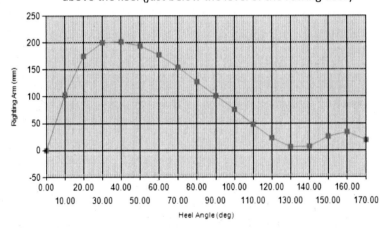

STABILITY CURVE
for loading of 800kg with the centre of gravity at 0.47m above the keel (just below the level of the rowing deck)

Fig. 2 The graph shows that irrespective of the boat's tilt (angle of 0-180 degrees), forces will act on it which will right it – with the keel pointing downwards. These forces will be strongest when the tilting angle is about 30-40 degrees and weakest when it's about 130-140 degrees.

Our idea was to organise a capsizing test for the boat in front of the Maritime Administration agency inspectors on Pancharevo Lake, but they thought that this would be a waste of time and even reprimanded us for launching the boat on the lake. We'd done it to show them that the boat was at least seaworthy, but we had to lift it out so they could take its exact measurements.

After the Maritime Administration agency inspectors had conducted their inspection of the boat, the trainer who had promised to assist us in its launch and testing with the crane, warned us not to come back to Pancharevo Lake with the boat because we were hampering the training of rowers from the sporting clubs. We tried to explain to him that the lake is public property and for this reason anyone who wanted to, should be able to use it. We were aware about the concerns that during the training sessions the academic boats move at a high speed and are not very manoeuvrable, which could be a determining factor in an incident. The rowers in these boats have their back to the direction of travel and if they didn't notice us and crashed into our boat or we bashed into theirs, the consequences would be very unpleasant, and the clubs could not afford to lose or be continually repairing damaged boats.

Following significant negotiations, the Maritime Administration agency issued us with a Certificate of Registry for NEVEREST with a Burgas licence number Bs 2711 and a Safety Navigation Certificate consonant with Ordinance No. 68 – for Region I-C up to 12 nautical miles. Max and Lara proudly stuck the name and registration number on both sides of the boat's prow.

In the evening we set off a red parachute rocket and lit a red hand-held flare in front of our house in Sofia to celebrate the boat's registration and to test this signalling equipment. Mylène had told us that some of her flares hadn't worked as they should, so we wanted to check that everything was fine with those we had bought. The parachute rocket flew up hundreds of metres above the city and lit up the sky bright red – just like a New Year firework, after which it fell slowly in a great parabola. The hand-held flare lit up with such blinding red over a period of 60 seconds, that it was impossible to look at it even for a second, and after that it went out on its own – just as expected. Everything looked in order, but we had to be very careful not to burn ourselves with this signalling equipment, if we ended up having to use them at sea.

These two means of signalling are used if a crisis happens at sea – if you need to send out SOS signals and seek rescue. Nevertheless, it had become traditional for ocean rowers to light up such flares before setting foot on land, after they had succeeded in crossing the ocean. My soul was raging with conflicting thoughts – on the one hand, I hoped that we wouldn't have to use them on our voyage, on the other hand, I couldn't wait to light them at the successful end of our ocean crossing. In the end I was simply grateful that we had the opportunity and privilege to plunge into such a great adventure, which doubtlessly would put our strength, mind and intellect to the many tests. It would make life infinitely more interesting.

Chapter 8

TRAINING SESSIONS ON ISKAR LAKE
AUGUST - SEPTEMBER 2020, MAX

As we were unable to train on Pancharevo Lake, which as it happens was too small anyway, we decided to continue our training on Iskar Lake – 30 kilometres from Sofia. Our first session was on the 20th of August 2019 and went on for about four hours. I rowed first for two hours, followed by my father. NEVEREST moved more quickly and easily than I expected. That being said, the boat was not fully loaded and there were no waves or strong wind to contend with.

The second session on the lake was even shorter, because the footplate bought from Rannoch Adventure which we tied our feet to while we were rowing, was mounted on a carbon fibre tube which broke into bits with the first stronger thrusts of the oars. Again there were no big waves or strong wind, so the pressure on her could have scarcely been too great. We had to row back, without our feet being fastened, which took a long time, because we were unable to use the sliding seat effectively. It's good that the tube broke in training and not in the ocean; if it had, it would have been really difficult if not impossible for us to get back without help from others.

We got home and mended the footplate, changing the carbon fibre tube with a metal one. To be quite sure it was strong, we drove it into a second metal tube on the upper part of the footplate and put in an additional metal tube in its lower part. It might seem this was a lot of tubes, but we wished to strengthen the structure for any eventuality, so it would endure every burden during the training and the ocean voyage.

This incident showed us what unfortunate surprises could happen during the voyage. Almost every element of the boat could break, which would make the voyage difficult if not impossible. That's why, when something broke or needed changing or strengthening, we told ourselves we'd escaped yet one more potential problem which would have been far more critical if it happened during the voyage.

That being said, although we knew we had to take with us spare parts, tools and handy materials for repairs, there was no way to insure ourselves against every potential problem. Instead of discouraging us however, these malfunctions stimulated us to use our heads even more intensively in the following stages of the boat's preparation and equipping, so as to reduce the chances that similar technical failures would force us to abort the voyage. That's why many times, I mentally passed my eyes over every device and every part of the boat, assessing whether it was at risk of breaking or failing. This process gave me additional assurance, as it pushed back all thoughts of failure.

It's amazing to think that at no point during the build, the training or the testing of our boat, did I think of giving up. This to some extent was down to the fact that I had promised myself that I would not set out if I was not 100% sure that everything on board was working as it should. When obstacles appeared in our path, we didn't despair, we overcame them and this felt like we were one step closer to being fully prepared.

Our most gratifying session on Iskar Lake was on the 28th of September 2019, when we launched the boat before sunrise and took it out after sunset. In the first hours after sunrise, the temperature was about 0 degrees Celsius and the lake was shrouded in mist which crept over the water and limited visibility to several metres. So as I rowed, I did not see the bank and I imagined we were in the North Atlantic Ocean already. It was like a fairy tale.

IN THE BLACK SEA
SEPTEMBER 2019, STEFAN

On the 7th of September 2019 we launched NEVEREST into the sea for the first time. We started out from the port of Burgas on the Black Sea having decided to row for 24 hours. We set off in the late afternoon, without having a specific destination point. The Black Sea is well known for the fact that when the wind blows, short steep waves rise up which are particularly unpleasant for small yachts and seafaring vessels. From the moment we left the harbour we were buffeted by a head wind which gradually strengthened. Soon night fell and we had only travelled 5 nautical miles from the port and not more than 1 nautical mile from the shore! The headwind mercilessly shoved us backwards and we realised that we were getting terrifyingly close to the shore, where beaches alternated with rocks. When the wind blew straight at the prow, we could row with both oars, but almost every minute the prow deviated to the left or right. Then the wind struck the side wall of the cabin and if the rower didn't take immediate counteraction, NEVEREST quickly turned perpendicular to the waves. The boat began to rock furiously, the oars stabbed and left the water almost uncontrollably, bashing into the rower's legs and there was a real danger of the oars or the oarlocks breaking, of the rower getting injured or even of the boat capsizing. So every time the boat's prow diverted from the direction of the headwind, we had to furiously row with just one oar, in order to return the boat to its original position. We struggled with this wind the whole night, and we took turns rowing every two hours – as we'd planned. It was scary, especially when we were approaching a big ship – we couldn't judge whether it was moving or at anchor. We tried contacting it by radio, but no one answered. There were no other ships close by and our radio transmissions were met by complete silence. When we had no choice but to pass quite close by the ship, we saw that it was at anchor.

The next morning, after we turned around, it only took a few hours rowing with the wind behind us to get back to Burgas harbour. We were drooping from exhaustion. Rowing six two-hour shifts with two-hour breaks and against the wind, turned out to be harder than I had imagined. We weren't used to sleeping intermittently and apart from that, the fear of being wrecked on the rocks had drained much of our energy. Although we had enough food on board we couldn't wait to get back on dry land and sit down at one of the cosy Burgas harbour restaurants and order the entire menu.

We contacted the harbour tower when we were a hundred metres from it and realised that our radio was actually working, however in the next outings we again had problems contacting other seagoing vessels and marinas. In the end, to our shame, we discovered that we hadn't installed an external antenna for the radio transmitter. This was the reason it only worked when we were really close to another radio.

When the time came to take NEVEREST out of the water, a new surprise awaited us – it turned out that at the end of the concrete ramp, down which small vessels were launched, the sea had eroded the shore and it had become too steep. For this reason, at the end of the ramp, NEVEREST's trailer sank deep and got wedged among the rocks. I tried to free it with the car, engaging the gears forward and reverse and turning the wheels left and right, but it did not budge – as if it had been cemented to the bottom. Max grabbed some goggles, stripped off to his boxers and jumped into the water. After he'd looked at the situation under the water, he began to pull, shove and lift the trailer by hand, until he freed it from the trap. After that there was no way we were not going to order the entire menu at the harbour fish restaurant and we almost managed to eat all of it.

IN THE AEGEAN SEA
NOVEMBER 2019 AND FEBRUARY 2020, MAX

On the 9th of November 2019, we tried out NEVER-EST in the Aegean Sea around Nea Potidea in Halkidi-ki, Greece having decided to row for 24 hours again. We knew that it would be fun and interesting as well as exhausting – this was still serious training. We arrived at the harbour the previous evening and decided to sleep in the cabin, to see how it felt. It was pretty tight, in that it was no wider than a single bed, but nevertheless it was bearable.

Our idea was to circle Kassandra – one of the peninsulas of Halkidiki. At its northern point, exactly where we launched the boat at Nea Potidea, there was a narrow channel, which actually cut through the natural peninsula and formed an artificial island. There was a weak wind and very small waves, so everything went smoothly during both the day and night. After almost 12 hours however, we'd travelled less than half the distance and my father suggested I make the decision whether to continue and finish our circumnavigation, which would have perhaps taken us 30-35 hours or to turn back and row the 24 hours we'd planned for. I judged it would be better that we turn around and go back to Nea Potidea in the planned 24-hour timeframe. I made this decision for a number of reasons. Firstly, due to the potential adverse conditions which would have hindered our progress if we chose to continue; secondly, we were still in training and getting used to the boat; thirdly, I did not want to rely on another boat having to tow us to shore; and lastly, I felt quite unwell and utterly exhausted which may well have been the factor that tilted the scales towards this decision.

We returned to the Aegean Sea on the 29th of November 2019, this time to Nea Peramos. We'd decided to carry out a few capsizing and self-righting tests of the boat in the marina there and afterwards to row round the island of Thasos in 48 hours. Again we slept on board the evening before setting out and we'd already begun to get used to the tight and rather stifling cabin. In the morning we tied a rope to the cleats, pulled it under the boat and wound it round the crane-winch, to apply the test. We were shocked when the boat capsized with its keel upwards, it froze in that position and did not right itself on its own, as it was supposed to do. My father immediately stripped to his boxers and jumped into the water, in spite of the temperature being certainly quite a lot below 20 degrees Celsius. After all he had swum the English Channel and he smugly announced that the temperature was wonderful.

The problem was serious; the boat did not flip back over, no matter how hard my father rocked it. He'd put his feet into the drain-holes on one side of the boat and with his entire weight pressing downwards, he tried jerking the boat to help it right itself. Finally he scrambled over the boat's hull, grabbed the rope, with which the winch had capsized the boat, and hung towards the opposite side. This made the boat flip over, but, because it had spent several minutes upside down, about 20 litres of water had leaked into the cabin. Fortunately, it had not damaged the electrical system or the electronics, but later we had to establish where the water had entered and to plug the holes. I knew that a 48-hour trip around Thasos awaited us and the last thing I wanted was a flooded cabin and faulty appliances. We bailed out the water from the cabin and set off.

The rowing was smooth and pleasant. When we began approaching Thasos, night fell and apart from the island lights flickering in the gloom we noticed a thread of lights directly ahead. Most probably they came from fishing boats out in the night. The thread of their lights were several kilometres long and we wondered whether to go round them, so as not to get tangled in their nets, or to try to pass through them. At the middle of the thread there was a big space – about a kilometre wide, and we decided to pass through there. When we got close to the fishing boats we noticed that some of the lights were moving faster than others, and when we got even closer, we saw that apart from the fishing boats there were objects floating in the water, like traps with strong searchlights, pointing downwards. Every searchlight was fastened to the top of a separate float, built over two big metal cylinders, and it moved with the wind independently to the fishing boats. Because the whole of this flotilla was moving to a large extent uncontrolled and perpendicular to our course, as we tried to pass through the boats and the traps, I felt fearful that we would collide with something hard and break or damage the boat. When you row with your back to the direction of travel, you cannot see at all what is floating in front of the boat. The only way to do that is to stop rowing, stand up and look over the cabin. Twice we passed fishing boats by some dozen metres and we tried to engage their crews, to learn what they were fishing – sea bream, sea bass, octopus? However, they didn't understand English, Bulgarian, German, Russian or Portuguese, and we didn't speak Greek, so we got nowhere.

After we passed the fishing boats, the wind and waves grew stronger and not much further on we saw a large motorboat approaching us with a bright searchlight. This turned out to be the coast guard from Kavala, who the fishermen had probably called up. The coast guards were quite amazed at what we were doing in a rowing boat in the middle of the night in such a place. It was as if they couldn't believe we were training for a transatlantic ocean crossing. From friends who have houses and boats in Greece, we'd heard that they impose fines somewhat arbitrarily and we expected they would fine us for something. They told us that according to Greek law, we had no right to row more than one nautical mile from the shore. They announced that we had to immediately make for the nearest harbour on Thasos and continue our rowing the following morning. My father calmly explained that if we were to have a minimal chance of crossing the Atlantic in our boat, we had to train without interruption at least a few days and nights and that we would keep to one nautical mile from the island, while we circled it, even though our boat's Safety Navigation Certificate states that we can row up to 12 nautical miles offshore. The waves were smacking our boat and that of the coast guard so strongly that we could barely keep them from colliding. Bearing in mind that the motorboat's hull was made of metal and that a satellite antenna and a GPS device were fastened over our boat close to their boat, we pleaded with the coast guard to inspect our documents more swiftly and let us get on our way. They turned out to be reasonable and did as we asked.

We continued our circuit through calm waters, almost to the end of the second night, when a storm whipped up, making it impossible to keep to any course by rowing except with the wind behind us, which would have sent us too far east of the island. So we decided to try our Jordan series drogue anchor. Its casting took less than a minute; the boat turned in the direction of the wind and its rocking significantly decreased. We were so tired from the last 40 hours of rowing, that both of us jumped into the cabin and almost immediately fell asleep. When we woke up about two hours later, the storm had passed and the boat was rocking gently in the waves. It took a couple of minutes to pull the anchor back into the boat and we carried on with our circuit.

Then the wind changed direction however, and began pushing us towards the island. Just a few more nautical miles and we'd have circled it, but we began to get terrifyingly close to land. It was complete darkness, with the exception of a few lights on the shore which seemed to be positioned at considerable distance from one another – it wasn't clear whether there was land jutting out to sea between them, towards us. If there were rocks close to the shore, we were in danger of crashing. One minute my father was looking at the chartplotter, the next he was peering at the outline of the shore in the darkness and he reassured me that in spite of us getting close to the island, we were running parallel to it. According to the chartplotter we were about half a nautical mile off the coast, but I wasn't entirely reassured, because when we were rowing close to Nea Peramos the previous day, from time to time the chartplotter falsely indicated that we were a few hundred metres inland, in spite of us actually being a few hundred metres off shore in the sea!

Rowing backwards, when there's the cabin behind you, limits your vision, like walking blindfolded. I put all my strength into rowing hard to get around the island and not too much later we passed to the other side. At last I could take a breather from the worry and the intensive rowing.

In the final few hours, an even stronger wind blew up and built up bigger waves but this time they were rolling in our direction, so we flew back to Nea Peramos at a speed we had never reached until then and somehow we finished our circuit around Thasos in 48 hours exactly as we had planned.

I have to admit that after each of our 12, 24, or 48-hour voyages, I felt infinitely tired as if I'd reached almost the end of my strength, especially after rowing around Thasos. It was as if all energy reserves in my body had been depleted and I was as hungry as a bear. After each of these rowing sessions, immediately after mounting the boat on the trailer, we would take off the rudder, tie up the oars, gather all the bits and bobs in bags and put them in the car, before rushing off to find the first restaurant. My father would then leave it to me to order whatever food, in whatever quantity I desired. Close by Iskar Lake as well as near the marinas in Burgas and Nea Peramos we managed to find unpretentious little restaurants with small menus, and I ordered plates of pretty much everything – as though there were five or six people around the table, not just two. During such exhausting rowing, food definitely motivated me to reach shore as quickly as possible and helped me cope with great physical burdens.

After our circuit of Thasos we also found a cosy local restaurant, we ate for a long time and assessed the experience, full of satisfaction that we'd managed a greater number of two-hour rowing shifts, that we'd overcome unexpected problems, that we didn't need to be rescued and that NEVEREST was a fantastic boat.

PROBLEMS WITH RIGHTING THE BOAT
FEBRUARY 2020, STEFAN

After the euphoria following our row round Thasos island had passed, we realised that we'd hit a wall. The problem of the boat not automatically righting itself was so great that it undermined the whole expedition. We could not set out to cross the ocean if we could not solve this issue somehow. If the two of us were in the cabin at the time of a storm and the boat capsized, no matter how much we rocked it from the inside, we wouldn't be able to exert as much force over it as I had in the first test in Nea Peramos, where I was standing outside on the drain-holes with all my weight. The water would gradually fill the cabin, and then the electrical system could break down irreparably or we ourselves could freeze. We would hardly drown in the cabin, because we'd open the hatch and swim out. In a strong storm though, we could be carried away from the boat and not be found in time, even if we managed to send out a signal for help from the EPIRB or the PLB.

I was convinced that we'd find a solution. I felt that we were like lions in a circus, who had to jump through hoops, where after each jump the circus handlers made the tricks more difficult – either setting fire to the hoop, fixing sharp knives into it, or setting up two-three hoops in a line, through which the lions had to jump in one go. Together with Phil Morrison, Stoyan Voivodov, Nikolay Djambazov and other friends and acquaintances, we began to collectively work our grey cells to find a solution.

The first idea that occurred to us was to put in a second, smaller hatch in the cabin, which would be positioned so that it would be above the water, irrespective of whether the boat was bottom-up or bottom-down. We watched the video of the capsizing tests with the crane many times and it seemed to us that we could put such a hatch on one side in the centre of the cabin. But so that it didn't let in water, such a hatch was likely to be really heavy. Also, though I was ready to leave the cabin during a storm, this wouldn't be wise, because the waves could sweep me far from the boat before I was able to tie myself to it. With the boat rocking during a storm, water could burst in through the open hatch, even when it was positioned above the waterline in a calm sea. And last but not least – we'd read about some ocean rowers, whose boats had been capsized many times during the same storm and the thought of depending on just the rower's strength to right the boat – weighing more than a ton in storm conditions, again and again, did not seem a reasonable solution.

The second idea was to cut away the roof of the cabin and the aft hold and build them higher so that when the boat capsized, they would have more volume and act like bigger balloons, on top of which the boat would not stay for more than a few seconds before automatically righting itself, bottom-down. Phil did some calculations and we saw that such an addition would entail too great an increase of the boat's proportions above the water. In this situation it would be much harder to fight the wind when it blew from any direction except from the stern. When I went to San Sebastián de la Gomera to look over the 35 boats competing in the Talisker Whisky Atlantic Challenge, I'd seen a boat with quite high cabins, fore and aft, and I noticed that it visibly rocked more than the others and tilted in one direction when the wind was blowing from the side, which meant the rower would have to strain, with one oar sunk deep into the water and the other scarcely reaching the surface. We decided this idea wasn't very practical either.

The third idea was to install a fixed keel-board (see figure 3) on the end of which we'd fix a keel-bulb as a counterweight, so that if the boat capsized, it would only take a little shaking to move the centre of its weight to one of the sides to right the boat again with its bottom pointing downwards. According to Stoyan, this bulb had to weigh about 60 kilograms. Phil again got to work with his calculations and asked me to send him a chart with the storage of all the heavier items on the boat, including the chargeable batteries, the watermaker, the two drogues, the traditional anchor, the water reserves, food provisions, etc. I had to tell him the weight of every single object and its position in centimetres of length and width, from a single reference point on the boat, which Phil had specified. He calculated that if a bulb weighing 80 kilograms was fixed at 40 centimetres below the keel, it would solve the capsizing problem, even if both rowers were locked in the cabin. Of course, the same result could be achieved with a lighter bulb and a longer keel-board. The installation of a keel-board and bulb however, would lead to some big disadvantages: its weight and its resistance in the water would slow the boat down (and we still hoped to set a speed record). Launching and lifting the boat out of the water would be much harder – the keel-board would have to be removable. Otherwise we'd have to lift and load the boat on the trailer with a crane. Moreover, there was the danger that with any rocking of the boat, the link between the hull and the keel-board and bulb would crack and water would flood into the cabin. We continued to seek more alternatives.

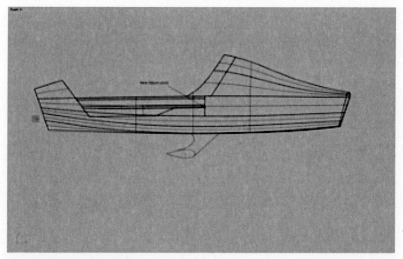

Fig. 3 A keel-board with a bulb

The fourth idea was to install heavier ballast on the inside of the hull – for example, steel (which is about eight times heavier than the same volume of water) or lead (which is 11 times heavier than the same volume of water). In this way we'd avoid most of the problems linked to the keel-board and bulb. Phil calculated that the weight of this ballast would have to be over 100 kilograms, but if such a weight were added to the boat, it would sink so deep that the waterline would go above the level of the basin under the rower's seat. There are four drain holes in that basin, whose function is to let the seawater from waves breaking over the deck go back under the boat. Thus, if NEVEREST lay too deep, the water would flood in from below through these drain holes, continually drenching the rower. This additional water onboard, would also weigh and slow down the boat considerably. Sadly, once again we had to dismiss the idea.

There was not even a single moment though, when we thought about starting the construction from scratch or giving up. We continued to bang our heads together. Nikolay Djambazov was frustrated with Phil's 'faulty' boat design, but I regarded the situation as just another hoop we had to jump through and another learning curve. In all honesty, the fault lay somewhat with us, as we had constructed the boat a few centimetres wider because of the stringers with which we'd rendered the curve of the hull, and we'd lifted the deck a few centimetres higher than Phil had planned so we would have a little more storage space. We assured Phil we weren't shy of hard work and if we had to rebuild the boat, we'd rebuild it as many times as necessary. If we didn't have the strength (mental and physical) to do the additional work, how would we find the strength to row across a whole ocean?

Finally, the fifth idea came – from Phil, who suggested that if we cut two channels, along the boat's sides, with which to lower the level of the deck this might possibly solve the problem. He told us that the boats he had designed for Rannoch Adventure had such channels, but in the beginning he'd decided to spare us these, to make the homemade construction easier. The rationale was as follows: in order to right the boat when it capsized with its keel pointing upwards, one of the sides, along with part of the deck and hold under it had to dip underwater, passing through the lowest point, where the boat's keel is found in its normal position, and after that emerging up above the water on the other side. The larger the hold spaces, however, the bigger the water displacement. As we had made them a few centimetres wider and taller, their volume was slightly greater than what Phil had foreseen. After significant discussion, we calculated with him that if we left the deck on both sides of the rower at 14 centimetres as we had built it, and lower the rest of the deck by 14 centimetres down the sides, we'd get rid of about 100 litres of volume from the storage holds on each side of the boat. After we cut these channels, we could expect either side, along with parts of the deck and storage holds below it to help right the boat with ease. Think of those inflatable bananas which speed boats pull after them and which carry five to ten people. If you reduce the volume of such an object by 100 litres, it would be enough for less people sitting on it to sink it below the water.

The last idea seemed logical; it lacked the serious inadequacies of the previous four ideas. Also, if the eight storage holds under the deck had lower ceilings, there would be no need to fix the items we were going to store in them to the floor, in order to keep the boat's centre of gravity lower, which was important so as to achieve self-righting. Cutting out parts of the deck, we'd also be getting rid of one or two kilograms from the boat's weight, which is always welcome. If we had smaller storage holds, we'd be more economical with the items we'd be taking with us on the voyage, and thus be lighter and quicker, a win-win. As they say, every cloud has a silver lining.

I rolled up my sleeves, grabbed the angle grinder and started cutting the deck of the boat, telling Max that with angle grinder moves like these, some Bulgarians used to cut the roofs off their Trabant cars and turn them into convertibles! The boat began to look like it had a few months earlier – without part of the deck, without hold hatches and covered in fine fibreglass dust. We again fell to cutting sheets of fibreglass, laminating, painting, bolting down the hatches and fixing various parts to the boat's deck and sides. I'd already developed an allergy to the lamination and the skin on my wrists again got covered in rashes and started peeling. However, I gritted my teeth and don't remember complaining.

On the 22nd of February we again drove the boat to Nea Peramos on the Aegean Sea, to carry out new capsizing tests with the crane and to row another 24 hours. My heart sank when the crane began to lift one side of the boat. This time it had to tilt it at 90 degrees or more before the boat went bottom up. Seconds passed, which seemed like hours to me.

The boat stayed bottom up over the calm water. This time, however, I didn't jump in to right it, but lightly tugged the rope, which was tied to the prow and it righted itself on its own. Hurrah!

We decided to carry out a second test, this time with Max inside the cabin, fastened with belts round his chest and waist, which we'd installed to keep us fixed to the floor while we slept through big storms. The crane lifted the boat and capsized it so that again it was left bottom up. I shouted to Max to rock it. He took a couple of seconds to undo the belts, but after that he moved from right to left and the boat righted itself, bottom down. Afterwards, he told me that it wasn't scary but, while the boat was capsized, he saw how a little water had begun to seep through the cabin hatch.

We decided that the tests were a success. For the boat to capsize in the ocean it would have to be hit by a pretty big wave, and with the presence of such big waves, it wouldn't be bottom up for long. Max and I love physics and I reminded him of a high school lesson in which they'd explained the difference between stable and unstable balance. If, for example, you put a tennis ball into the bottom of a salad bowl, it would be in a stable equilibrium in that if you push it, it'll bounce up and down the walls of the bowl but it will return to the bottom. If, however, you turn the bowl upside down, and put the ball on top and push it lightly, the ball will roll down the wall of the bowl and won't return – this is unstable equilibrium. Following this logic, if the boat turned bottom up in the ocean, it would be in an unstable equilibrium and as we established in the last two tests, it would need just a little rocking to right it.

NEW PROBLEMS
MARCH 2020, MAX

We noticed that on each outing, a little water gathered in the bottom of the holds. We thought there was no way it could have penetrated the hull, since we'd put on so many coats of fibreglass, resin and paint, inside and out! According to various people we talked to on this topic, it was most likely down to condensation of moisture in the air touching the walls of the boat. We discovered that because of such condensation, some ships had actually sunk. Modern ships are equipped with electric pumps that continuously suck out water from their holds and dump it overboard.

On the recommendations of Nikolay Djambazov and Stoyan Voivodov, we insulated the cabin with six-centimetre fibre polymer panels and three-millimetre sheets of cork, not only to avoid condensation in the cabin, but to decrease the chance of the boat sinking if it filled up with water. With this insulation we hoped to better protect our sleeping quarters from the cold during our voyage across the North Atlantic; to make the walls softer, so as to avoid bad injuries from knocks when the boat was being tossed by stormy waves; and of course, to make the cabin cosy! After all, it was going to be our home for months on end.

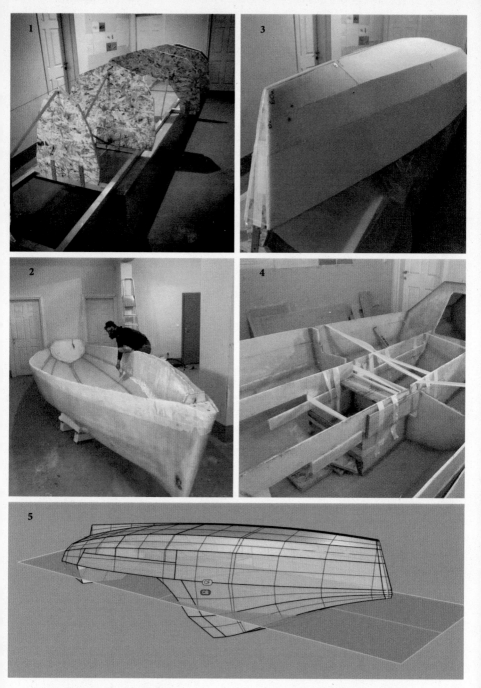

1. Temporary chipboard bulkheads
2. Laminating with epoxy resin, strand mat and fibreglass cloth
3. The hull from light porous panels
4. 13 waterproof compartments to ensure the boat will not sink
5. Calculations for self-righting the boat after capsizing

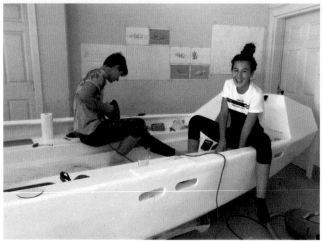

Lara helps with the installation of the hatches

Application of the polishing paste

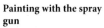

Painting with the spray gun

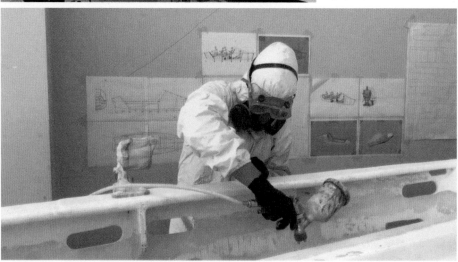

Victoria Dimitrova, nine months pregnant, teaches us to row on the ergometers

First Aid course

The 1.5-square metre cabin with the navigation and communications devices

EPIRB, PLB, satellite hotspot, satellite phone, VHF radio

Raw bars, sweets, protein bars, dried fruit, cheese, biscuits, lyophilized meals, etc.

Training in the Aegean Sea

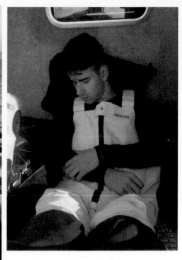

A snooze between
rowing shifts

NEVEREST departs
from Sofia to Portugal

With Ralph Tuijn before the voyage

The last capsizing
test in Portimão

Jenny and NEVEREST the day before the departure from Portimão, Portugal

Chapter 8

While we were in the middle of rebuilding the boat to fix the capsizing problem, I invited Maxim Behar and his wife Veneta Pisarska to dinner at our home. Maxim and I had known each other for more than ten years and we had served for a few years on the Board of Directors of Junior Achievement Bulgaria – a non-profit organisation, focused on youth education. The global Junior Achievement organisation had reached over 80 million youngsters around the world and in Bulgaria more than 2000 teachers, and 4000 volunteer consultants had taught over 200 000 pupils through many interesting educational courses. Maxim is founder and leader of the M3 Communications Group – one of the most successful PR companies in the world, he has written many books, received countless international PR awards and has taken on a succession of responsible roles in international organisations.

We shared with Maxim our plans to cross the Atlantic in a rowing boat and our wish to support the

NEVEREST

publicity and exposure of the Ministry of Health's Yes! To life! campaign through which the lives of many Bulgarians needing organ transplants could be saved. We sought his advice about the best way to reach more potential donors through traditional and social media platforms. Maxim immediately declared that he'd be glad to help pro bono. He advised us to create pages of the project on Facebook and Instagram, where we'd need to continually post news about the progress of building the boat and the ultimate voyage across the ocean, both in Bulgarian and in English.

Maxim and his colleagues from M3 sent press releases about our imminent voyage to the Bulgarian media which prompted a wave of interviews on TV, radio, online and in printed media. We only accepted interviews on the condition that we'd discuss not only the voyage across the ocean, but also the Yes! To life! campaign. All journalists reacted positively and this convinced us that we'd chosen the right cause to support and publicise with our voyage.

Until this moment, Max hadn't given many interviews and he was worried about speaking in front of a microphone and camera, but all of the journalists were exceptionally well disposed and the interviews with them passed pleasantly and smoothly. There were no questions that we tried to avoid and we were pleased that the subject of organ donation received the ever sought after publicity. It was fantastic to read the public's comments that were overwhelmingly positive and that more and more people announced they had made the decision to become organ donors after they died. So in what was only a matter of days, our plans for our forthcoming voyage, known by only a few close relatives and friends, suddenly became public knowledge. This brought about a variety of reactions, the overwhelming number of which were encouraging and charged with positive energy. Of course, there were comments that we were 'going to our deaths'; that we 'didn't know what we were doing'; along with opinions from "experts" that such a voyage could not be accomplished for whatever "objective" reasons. There were some fun comments of the sort "Dear me, now I've got to worry about these guys as well. So much better if they'd announced the voyage after they'd done it!"

Chapter 10

Our preparation for the North Atlantic route from Newfoundland Island, Canada to the Isles of Scilly, UK was going full speed. We'd been taking cold showers since the summer, to harden ourselves up – with the coming of autumn and winter the temperature of the water gradually fell and we increased our time under the shower. My father had a conditioning routine which he'd worked out back at the time when he'd been preparing to swim the English Channel. In the beginning you count to 100 before applying the soap, and then to 300 while you wash off the soap under the cold stream of the shower. Every time you raise the count little by little and gradually you reach 500 before and 1500 after soaping. He thought that more than this would lead to using too much water. During the winter months under these cold showers, my blood would begin to roar, my heart would pound furiously and my skin would turn bright red.

We bought detailed maps and navigational charts of the coastlines of Newfoundland and Scilly. We found a transport company to carry NEVEREST in a container from the port of Burgas to that of St. John's, Newfoundland, from where we thought to launch.

The coronavirus pandemic had begun to dig deeper in the world and more and more countries took on stricter measures to constrain it. To our regret, Canada announced that it wouldn't allow foreigners entry to their territory until the end of June 2020. If we had to wait until the beginning of July to enter the country and then to prepare the final provisions and get the boat ready for launch, and to hope for a suitable meteorological window for setting off, it would certainly not happen until the middle of July or later. That wasn't optimal as the preferred period for launch was the first half of June. We would have had an even bigger problem if we'd sent the boat to St. John's and in the meantime, Canada decided to lengthen its prohibition to the end of July or August. This meant we'd have missed the chance of rowing over the summer. We researched the Canadian law about exceptional circumstances related to COVID-19 and we found out that it made an exemption for the entry of a number of categories of foreigners into the country, including:

- *Crew on any plane, train or marine vessel*
- *People who are making necessary medical deliveries required for patient care, such as cells, organs, tissues, blood and blood products.*

We got in touch with the immigration authorities in Newfoundland, but they answered that they could not take a decision to allow us into Canada and advised us to turn to the Canadian Embassy in our country. There is no Canadian Embassy in

Bulgaria, so we wrote a detailed letter to the Ambassador of the Canadian Embassy in Romania, which was also responsible for Bulgaria. They answered that they'd examined the case carefully, but regrettably felt we did not fall into the exemption categories.

We wrote twice to the Chief Public Health Officer of Canada, who according to Canadian law could personally permit foreigners' entry to the country in exceptional circumstances. Sadly we didn't get a response. Thus, it became necessary for us to seek alternative routes across the Atlantic ocean. We could have panicked, but there would be no point; this unforeseen obstacle was completely beyond our control, we had to accept and adapt.

A new idea blossomed: to row the same route as that first voyage of Christopher Columbus, completed in 1492-1493 – from Palos de la Frontera, Spain to the island of San Salvador in the Bahamas, with one stop for the repair of one of three ships in the fleet in San Sebastián de la Gomera. Sadly though, at this particular moment in time, Spain was one of the European countries most affected by coronavirus and thus was also blockaded – even Spaniards were not allowed to travel between separate towns in their country.

Its neighbour, Portugal was managing better with coronavirus and they were expected at any moment to open their borders to Bulgarians. It occurred to us that another potential cross Atlantic route would be from Portugal to Brazil. Both my sister Lara and I were born in Brazil, but my family moved back to Bulgaria when I was three and a half, and my sister was younger than two years old so we had no memories of the country. My parents told me that I first spoke Portuguese, in spite of them always talking to me in Bulgarian and despite English being the language of instruction in our kindergarten. According to my parents this was down to my instinct for survival. I probably realised that if I spoke Bulgarian, I could only socialise with them, my parents; if I spoke English, I could only talk with the children and teachers in the kindergarten and my parents; if I spoke Portuguese, I'd be understood by everyone around me.

My mother and father adored Brazil. They first went to live in São Paulo for five months in connection with my father's work, which then took them to South Korea for another five months and then to London for nine months. They insisted on returning to Brazil and settled once again in São Paulo, this time for seven years. They crossed the length and breadth of this huge country, fell in love with the Portuguese language, Brazilian music and nature and to this very day they can't get enough of Brazilian culture. Thus, in conversations with my father about potential routes for our transoceanic voyage, the idea of rowing from Portugal to Brazil occurred to us. Although I had Bulgarian and Brazilian citizenship, I've always felt Bulgarian, but I was curious to again get to know the country I was born in.

We sent a letter to the Bulgarian Embassy in Lisbon, so we'd be better briefed of their position in the matter and to our joy, the Ambassador himself called us – Mr. Vasiliy Takev. He'd taken to heart our expedition and the Yes! To life! cause we were supporting, and undertook personally to inform us about the opportunity to launch from Portugal. It turned out that when he was the Ambassador of Bulgaria in Spain, he'd worked on a project for the opening of the first transplant centre in Bulgaria – this was made possible with the financial support of the King of Spain.

Ambassador Takev kept us in the loop in his discussions with the Portuguese Ministry of Foreign Affairs. At this particular moment in time, the country was slowly beginning to relax the restrictions for foreign access to its territory, but the rules, which were constantly changing, were very confusing. Just when we needed to travel to Portugal, it allowed access to the citizens of the Schengen area. Bulgaria was still not officially a part of this area, but fulfilled the criteria for entry. However strange it sounded to us, Ambassador Takev had got word-of-mouth confirmation from the Portuguese Ministry of Foreign Affairs that Bulgarians could travel to Portugal, albeit not by a direct flight, but with a change of planes in a Schengen country. I could not comprehend how this would have helped in the fight against the coronavirus, but for us this open door was welcome and we decided to make use of it.

Chapter 11

All ocean rowers we talked to, told us that during their voyages, they had one, or several, navigators back on land, who followed weather forecasts, warned of approaching storms and helped them with navigating the ocean. It turns out that, as on a mountain and so in the ocean, a straight line from A to B is not always the fastest route and we would soon learn this the hard way.

One of my friends – Todor Dimitrov, a.k.a. El Capitan, was a captain in the Bulgarian Navy and a teacher at the Military Academy G.S. Rakovski – the oldest military school in Bulgaria. Todor is one of the legendary Bulgarian long-distance runners who has participated in numerous marathons and ultramarathons, including the longest race in the world – Sri Chinmoy Self-transcendence 3100 mile race in New York. In 2019, together with him and another friend of ours, Dimitar Kyosev, we formed the Bulgarian Lions team and took part as the first Bulgarian team in the longest ultramarathon in the UTMB-PTL framework (Ultra Trail du Mont Blanc – Petite Trotte à Léon). It includes conquering 300 kilometres of mountain paths through the Alps and climbing over 25,000 metres – the equivalent of climbing on foot to the stratosphere. Although he loves orienteering and has taken part in many competitions, Todor did not offer himself up as an ocean navigator, but instead, his friend and fellow pupil from the Naval Academy – Captain Valeri Petrov. Valeri had sailed for about 20 years as a navigator and captain of big ships throughout the world and had passed through innumerable storms and hurricanes, some of which proved fatal for other ships. For some years he'd been the navigator of Seaborne Sojourn – one of the big cruise ships in the world, which mostly followed non-traditional routes to the fjords, the Arctic, the Antarctic, etc. Because his passengers were mostly older and quite demanding people, who did not especially welcome being rocked about on their cruises, Valeri had to master in depth, the theory and practice of meteorology and navigation, in order to keep the ship far away from storms.

Valeri was an exceptionally methodical, calm and responsible man. Even before our launch he managed to come to Sofia so we could get to know each other and to cast an eye over NEVEREST. Most of the time, he was sailing across the world and when he wasn't at sea, he lived with his family in Varna. He recommended a few books about meteorology to us, and readily discussed with us in detail the alternative routes. He didn't say that any of them were impossible, and shared with us his opinion on the pros and cons of each.

Jenny, my wife, was of course worried about everything and in every way tried to reduce the risks we were likely to run into on the voyage. Therefore, she made us search out ocean rowers who had rowed from Europe to South America and to get in touch with some of them to ask them about this route. We established that the Dutch rower, Ralph Tuijn had rowed five or six times from Portugal to French Guiana or Trinidad and Tobago and we decided to contact him. It turned out that he was the most experienced ocean rower, having crossed the Atlantic, Pacific and Indian oceans and travelled more nautical miles than anyone else – over 40,000. Ralph's first question to us was: "Why are you going to row in the hurricane season? No one does that!" We explained that we were still wondering which route to take, but we had to row in the summer because Max was in school through the rest of the year.

Ralph told us about the winds and currents he'd come across between Europe and South America. For him the easiest route was between Portugal and French Guiana. Ralph's day job was as a nurse and he clearly had an innate passion for helping people. In our very first conversation on the telephone, he suggested that he become our navigator and declared that he would do this completely for free. I began to explain that we already had a navigator and we wouldn't want to take up his valuable time, but Jenny and Max jumped off the sofa and interrupted me, saying that they'd be really happy for him to orientate and advise us, irrespective of which route we decided to take. Ralph stated that it was essential to have good navigators, even more than one, and he used several navigators on dry land during all of his transoceanic voyages.

CHOICE OF ROUTE
MAY 2020, MAX

My father again insisted I choose the route we would take. After some of the options fell by the wayside – for example, the Christopher Columbus route, because Spain was entirely closed for an indefinite period, we narrowed the choice to the following alternatives:

A) St. John's, Canada – The Isles of Scilly, UK

Distance: 1819 nautical miles (3369 kilometres) as the crow flies
Start: July 2020

Pros:
- Possibilities of a record for 'The youngest rower' and 'The fastest crossing'
- Shortest route

Cons:
- Uncertainty of permission to enter Canada
- Colder water

B) San Sebastián de la Gomera, Canary Islands – Antigua, Caribbean Islands, as competitors in the Talisker Whisky Atlantic Challenge or independently.
Distance: 2551 nautical miles (4724 kilometres) as the crow flies
Start: December 2020

Pros:
- Most favourable winds
- Rescue yachts of the competition organisers

Cons:
- Not such a big rowing adventure
- Possibly lengthier absence from school
- Minimal chance to set a record including missing out on 'The youngest ocean rower' possibility.

C) Portimão, Portugal – Fortaleza, Brazil
Distance: 2960 nautical miles (5482 kilometres) as the crow flies

Start: June 2020

Pros:
- Chances for records for 'The youngest rower', 'First boat with a pair of rowers from Europe to South America' and 'First rowing boat to cross the Atlantic from east to west entirely during the hurricane season'
- Finish in Brazil

Cons:
- Greater danger of storms and hurricanes
- Unfavourable winds and currents
- Longest route

In any case, our voyage with NEVEREST would be the first Bulgarian ocean rowing expedition and this filled me with pride and a sense of responsibility.

I chose the last route – from Portimão, Portugal to Fortaleza, Brazil. Firstly, for me it was important to finish our trip in Brazil, to visit my second motherland. Secondly, we'd heard that for most of the time we'd either have following winds or calm seas. In both cases that would be good for us because we'd tested the boat and knew that it moved relatively quickly even when there was no wind. We also knew that there was a big chance to encounter a hurricane or storm, but we had a plan to pass south of 'hurricane highway'. Therefore, I saw real potential in this route and thought it the right choice. It remained to be seen if I was right.

Chapter 12

THE FORECAST ACCORDING TO THE STARS
MAY 2020, STEFAN

I've never believed in astrology. When someone asks me what my star sign is, I often answer that I have no star sign, because I don't want to be pigeonholed with people born more or less at the same time in the year as me, and to have a prescriptive set of characteristics or lack of, simply because of the disposition of the stars at the time of my birth. I believed even less that the stars' disposition affects our everyday lives differently according to our star signs.

In contrast to me, however, Jenny sometimes lends an ear to astrologers and just a few weeks before our planned launch, had consulted with one of the most authoritative astrologers in Sofia about our upcoming expedition. After she'd made the necessary calculations and charts, the astrologer stated categorically that it would be entirely absurd for us to undertake such a voyage in the next few months. June and July were entirely unsuitable for Max because of some critical aspect of Uranus – the planet was going to enter Taurus and create a square with Max's moon – something which happened once in 85 years. As for me, the month of August was extremely unfavourable for such an undertaking, because of the Mars aspect – this on the other hand happened once in 27 years. Faced by such critical aspects, our intuition would partly fail and we wouldn't know what we were doing or how to escape critical situations. We'd be susceptible to incidents, cuts, bruises, sprains, problems with our vestibular apparatus, etc.

I was left speechless – how could I counter these arguments when I neither knew anything about astrology, nor believed in it. The only thing that occurred to me was to beg Jenny to talk to two more astrologers, as I reckoned that each one would say something different and in this way they'd refute each other. Jenny did so – she met and consulted with not two but three more astrologers to discuss the position of the planets, relative to the dates of our upcoming voyage – recording each conversation on her mobile phone. To my huge astonishment they came up with very similar concerns about Mars and Uranus and concluded that we'd chosen an extremely unsuitable time for the expedition.

Even so, there were some discrepancies between the astrologers' words, which to some extent threw into doubt the plausibility of their interpreted events. By now we'd been preparing this expedition for a year and a half and we'd accumulated confidence, purposefulness and determination, to manage anything that got in our way. We had a family discussion and decided that there'd never be ideal conditions or an ideal moment for our departure, for the greatest variety of reasons – some of them objective, some subjective, some supernatural – and we decided that there was no sufficiently serious reason to stop us setting out and bringing this voyage to a conclusion.

Chapter 13

The whole family – Max, Jenny, Lara and I, took a First Aid Course. We learnt how to treat wounds, bleeding, burns and broken extremities, how to help someone who has passed out or has hypothermia, how to administer mouth to mouth resuscitation and heart massage.

My brother Kalin Dimitrov – an orthopaedic traumatological surgeon of 20 years' experience in UMHATEM (University Multiprofile Hospital for Active Treatment and Emergency Medicine) N.I. Pirogov and UHAT (University Hospital for Active Treatment) Sofiamed, would be our expedition doctor. In his professional practice he had cured countless serious injuries and over the years had helped the family, relatives, friends and friends of friends to cope with all kinds of medical problems. With his colleagues in Sofiamed, he had even managed to sew a big toe into the place of an amputated thumb. With his help, we prepared a first aid kit for our voyage which was probably better equipped than

the kits on most commercial ships – it barely fitted into four bags with a total volume of over 20
litres. Before our setting out, he taught us how to
carry out injections on each other's hindquarters
and we even tried this in practice. A day or two before flying to Portugal, inadvertently I hit my face
with some pliers and tore the skin, presenting Max
with the chance to work on a bleeding wound in
real time.

In the previous 18 months we'd rowed on an ergometer over 7000 kilometres. Of those, 2500 were
in the gym at the beginning of our training with Victoria Dimitrova and 4500 at home because of COV-
ID-19. This distance was longer than our planned
route in the Atlantic. In the last 100 days, following the training programme Vicky had prepared for
us, we were training six days a week, sometimes in
two or three two-hour sessions every two hours.

On the recommendation of acquaintances and
strangers we got ourselves audiobooks and podcasts to listen to on the voyage. Some of Max's
friends had put together a flash drive with music
which we'd listen to on the boat. We downloaded
hundreds of hours of music onto our phones. We
feared that reading in a constantly rocking boat
would cause seasickness, but despite this, we took
a few books.

For days on end, Jenny and Lara carefully vacuum packed 140 food bags – one for each of us for
70 days. Every bag contained about 4650 calories.
Up to 1800 of these calories were in the form of
lyophilized (freeze-dried) meals, which were very
light, nourishing and varied – all kinds of pasta,
rice, meat and vegetable meals with Italian, Asian,

Mexican flavours, scrambled eggs, etc. Additionally, in each bag were 75 grams of nuts, 100 grams of dried fruit, protein bars and raw sweets, crackers and very rarely (to lift our spirits) some unhealthy but calorific chocolate dessert. In addition to the bags, we took 4 kilograms peanut butter, 3 kilograms Nutella, 4 kilograms powdered protein, 3 kilograms electrolytes, 5 kilograms apples, 5 kilograms oranges, about 100 energy gels, 4 packets of biscuits, scores of tortilla wraps instead of bread, 0.5 kilograms dried meat, 0.5 kilograms olives, etc. The weight of all the food was about 200 kilograms. It took us a whole day to load and arrange it on the boat along with all other necessities, spare parts, clothes, etc. Everything which we'd planned to take fortunately fitted into the boat.

We loaded NEVEREST onto a lorry from a transport firm with an electrifying name, Zhelyo Voivoda (Zhelyo the Warlord) and sent it directly to the little town of Portimão in Portugal. Along the way, customs officers on some border crossings stopped the lorry, thinking that there were narcotics in the packets of lyophilized food but the driver, with the resonating nickname of Petyo the Warlord, managed to convince them that there were no narcotics and thus avoided the full unloading and reloading of the boat.

PORTIMÃO
3 JUNE 2020, MAX

My father and I arrived in Portimão along with my mother and sister. We flew through Germany and Lisbon; luckily the pandemic travel restrictions did not hinder our passage or the transportation of NEVEREST. By coincidence Ralph had to go to Portimão at exactly the same time, to collect his car and trailer which he'd left there after his last voyage. This was a wonderful opportunity for him to carry out a detailed inspection of our boat and give us some final advice – like, for example, to tie the autopilot to the boat, so the waves that would surely wash over us didn't carry it away; to take belts, like the ones mountaineers use, to fasten ourselves to the boat by means of rope tied to the belt around our waists, instead of the safety jacket around the shoulders – which we had been doing up to this point; to stock up on a lot more wet wipes; to buy additional detailed maps of the northern coast of South America, which we could download on our phones, etc.

On the insistence of Ralph and my mother, we carried out more capsize tests with the crane in the water – this time the boat was fully loaded with my father and me inside in the cabin. We had to rock it left and right and it rolled back with its keel pointing down. We did the test twice, as it seemed to us that the first time the crane operator had helped us a little, as he had pulled up the rope with the crane. These capsize tests were pretty stressful and unpleasant because once we had loaded the boat with all the provisions, we didn't know how it would manage to return to its proper position; there was a chance that things wouldn't pan out as we had planned. Inside the cabin, when we were capsized, we fought a battle with time – the longer the boat stayed in this position, the more it filled with water, which would further hamper its self-righting. It was a relief that we managed to right it quickly and without losses.

The conversations with Ralph were very valuable and reassuring for us, and especially for my mother. Over the course of lunches and dinners at Portimão he told us about his voyages and narrow escapes in ocean rowing boats and answered all the questions that occurred to us.

In the last days before our start, it turned out that our brand new YB3 tracker, through which our navigators, family and friends could follow where we were, refused to transmit the coordinates of our position. The YB Tracking team reacted immediately and sent us a new tracker of the same model. A few weeks before that, our brand new Iridium GO! Hotspot also turned out to be faulty – it shut down multiple times while downloading a weather forecast. The PredictWind team also responded immediately and after we had sent them the problematic device to look at, they replaced it with a new one. Just before setting out, we became convinced that our satellite equipment was not very dependable – as we had already discovered. For this reason we took with us three different devices for two way communication – so we wouldn't lose contact with our land based team.

And so, after almost two years of preparation, at last we could set out on our voyage. Ocean rowers say that half the challenge is getting to the starting line. As I remember how many tens, if not hundreds of things we had to learn, think over, prepare, try out, change, reject, approve or work through, I understand what they mean. Even my mother seemed to be convinced that we were, if not fully, at least adequately prepared and confident in ourselves to set off.

Just before the launch, we used drawing pins to stick to the cabin walls a few pictures of our family, chosen by my mother, along with pictures of my cousins, Iva and Nikola, which they'd given us in Sofia. My little cousin, Iva, had drawn a picture of NEVEREST in the sea, which we also stuck on the wall. My aunt Galia had given us a small blessed icon with the figure of Saint Nicholas the miracle worker – protector of sailors and fishermen, which we stuck right over our pillows on the ceiling of the cabin.

Before leaving Bulgaria, some of our relatives and friends had written us letters and sealed them in envelopes, to be opened at the most difficult moments on the expedition. With all this support, we felt that we'd not be alone in any moment of our voyage and we were finally ready to launch into the ocean.

PART 2

VOYAGE

Chapter 14

Ralph insisted we choose the most favourable time for starting out – with a forecast of north winds for at least three to four days ahead, so we could put a safe distance between us and the shore. He told us that during the voyage we obviously wouldn't be able to choose the meteorological conditions, so it would be good if at least we had favourable weather in the first few days.

On the 27th of May 2020, a few weeks before our launch from Portimão, the ocean rower Milan Svetnik started out from New York towards Great Britain in his wonderful boat, Czechmate, manufactured by Rannoch Adventure. Three days later the wind cast him along with his boat on the Long Island shore. Fortunately, Milan got by with minimal injuries, and his boat – just with a broken rudder and a few little breakages, which he managed to repair in a few days. Milan was not only an experienced and hardened rower, but clearly strong psychologically; in spite of the unpleasant start he mobilised himself and launched again, this time from Long Island on the 7th of June 2020. Over 37 days and nights' struggle with changing winds, he managed to gain only 300 nautical miles east of land before returning unharmed to Long Island again, firm in his decision to start again a year later. On the 18th of May 2021, Milan set out again from New York, but sadly after 18 days and nights' struggle with ocean winds and waves, he decided to accept help from the US coast guard, which towed his boat back to Long Island once more.

The weather forecasts in the Portimão region changed every day, the wind direction was exceptionally unstable over the three or four days after we'd been completely ready to start, so every day Ralph recommended waiting for a better meteorological window. Finally, according to forecasts from PredictWind and Windy, the winds were expected to be suitable and the ocean – comparatively calm; it looked like a few days of favourable weather awaited us.

On the 14th of June 2020, a little after sunrise, NEVEREST set out on its first ocean voyage. Many friends and relatives wanted to see us off from the shore, but because of the coronavirus pandemic, which continued to spread like wildfire in Europe, it wasn't sensible to undertake unnecessary journeys. I promised myself that I would think of everyone who had supported us and without whose help we would scarcely have reached this moment.

When our boat left the shore, the two upright figures of Lara and Jenny remained on dry land. Around each of our wrists Lara had tied a blue thread and told us she was giving us her strength. Jenny hugged us one after the other, long and lovingly as she liked to do, and as only she could. As we drew further away, I thought of everything we'd lived through together, remembered the thousands of hours spent in the garage, the conversations, worries and thrills. I looked at the silhouettes of my beloved women and was filled with gratitude – for the chance to start this voyage and everything that awaited us. As the boat drew away from the shore, I shouted to them: "When we see each other next time, we'll have grown." I didn't just have Max in mind and not just physical growth; I was sure that this voyage would change us in many ways. And in this same spirit we'd stuck to the cabin hatch the slogan: 'Growth happens outside the comfort zone', which was a paraphrase of Tony Robbins' quote 'All growth starts at the end of your comfort zone.'

It was very early in the morning and the Portimão harbour border officials had not arrived at work. We decided that we wouldn't wait for them and we'd start out, because a few days earlier we had informed them of our intention to row to Brazil and Jenny was going to pop in to confirm our departure when the working day began. There was no need for stamps in our passports as Bulgaria, along with Portugal, is a member of the European Union.

Max took the first rowing session and we distanced ourselves from the Portimão harbour. The water was smooth as though we were on a lake. We travelled at about 2.5 knots (2.5 nautical miles an hour or 4.6 kilometres an hour). The sun shone pleasantly; there wasn't even one cloud in the sky; from the boat's sound system jolly music played; and I felt how with every oar-stroke we drew closer to Brazil. As always, we began to take turns on the oars every two hours.

FIRST DAY IN THE OCEAN
14 JUNE 2020, MAX

We'd decided to divide the unimaginably long distance we were about to cover into small stages, so we could focus on concrete foreseeable goals and feel that we were progressing. For the first day we had set three goals:

1. To distance ourselves by at least a few dozen nautical miles out on to the ocean, so the wind and waves wouldn't cast us back on shore.
2. Not to overburden ourselves, so as not to injure ourselves or burn out at the very start.
3. To be careful not to succumb to seasickness.

As far as goal number one was concerned, the distancing from the shore went like clockwork. After less than six hours though, a headwind built up, it was my turn to row and as my father looked at the chartplotter, he commented on the speed I was rowing at – it was slowly decreasing from 2.5 knots to 2 knots ... 1.5 knots... 1 knot and then to only 0.5 knots. My father thought it best for me to continue rowing and try to get further away from the shore, despite the low speed and my ever increasing efforts. Minutes later, however, he jumped out of the cabin and told me that the speed of travel relative to the earth continued to be 0.5 knots, but our course instead of being 230 degrees (southwest) had turned to 50 degrees (northeast) – i.e. despite me rowing with al-

most all my strength, the boat was going backwards
– to the northeast.

The first thing I thought was that we'd really let
down our trainer Vicky, all the participants in the
project and ourselves if, just a few hours after setting
out, we allowed the wind to push us back and wreck
us on the rocks.

We decided to cast the floating anchor. Up to this
moment we'd used only the Jordan series drogue,
suitable for strong following winds but now for the
first time we had to cast the para anchor which helps
against headwinds. It was tied to a lead rope, secure-
ly stored towards the prow, and as we'd see them do
on YouTube, we took the parachute out of its bag,
dropped it into the water on the windward side of
the boat and after it opened up, we slowly paid out
the 80-metre rope, until it tautened and the boat's
prow turned against the wind. Fortunately, after a
few hours the gusts died down and it was time for us
to row again.

Casting the floating anchor had been the easy bit –
we'd carried it out just like the textbook. Its retrieval
on board, however, proved to be a problem. The parachute had sunk directly below the boat and when
we tried to pull it up, it was as if we were pulling a
bucket of water, weighing more than a 100 kilograms,
from a well. We took turns on the rope, we pulled
together, we took turns again; there was no end to
the pulling. From time to time, when the boat rose
high up a wave, the rope slipped through our hands
and scraped our wet fingers, tearing at layers of our
softened skin. My father was worried we'd damage
our backs on the very first day and he already had
two herniated discs on his spine. At one moment we

wondered whether we shouldn't just cut the rope and be left with the second drogue, but we quickly rejected this idea and carried on with our re-enactment of the 'Grandpa pulling out the turnip' story. So in respect of goal number two, things were not going favourably.

To cap it off, goal number three wasn't a success on the very first day either. When I was in the cabin I felt so sick that I couldn't hold it and I threw up. I have to admit that during almost all our practice trips on the Black and Aegean seas, I succumbed to seasickness on the first day. Until this moment, we hadn't been on the water for more than two days at a time, so we didn't actually know whether my sea-sickness would pass after a few days or whether I would suffer five to ten days and get as thin as a rake before stabilising. There are some people who cannot get better at all and they have to be taken ashore – this has happened many times in the history of ocean rowing expeditions.

In our conversations with ocean rowers, we had gathered numerous pieces of advice on how to cope with seasickness. Vomiting on the ocean happens most often when the body feels that it's rocking and the eyes see a static picture – for example, when you are reading a book in the cabin. When you are seasick, the body is fooled to think that you have eaten rotten or poisonous food, so it triggers the emptying of the stomach as a defence reaction. The pieces of advice we decided to follow to avoid seasickness were:

- To eat very little before setting out, as well as during the first few days.
- In the beginning to wear a plaster behind our ears with an active substance which suppresses seasickness.

- To wear, for at least a few days, elastic wrist-bands, similar to those worn by tennis play-ers, but with a tiny plastic ball which the band squeezes to the inside of the forearm, at about three fingers above the wrist. Some experienced rowers had given us this recommendation, even though it wasn't entirely clear to us how pres-sure from this ball suppresses the symptoms of seasickness.
- To buy ourselves a device, looking like a wrist-watch, which has two electrodes on its side that touch the arm; they transmit electric waves, which suppress convulsions in the stomach.
- To take with us several kinds of pills for sea-sickness.

Anyway, we didn't use the device or the pills. Fortu-nately, I got by with just one vomiting episode at the beginning of our voyage and another couple during huge storms. My father on the other hand showed no signs of discomfort or difficulties with eating on the sea and never suffered from seasickness. In any event, I was happy for him and I only had to worry about my own condition.

Chapter 15

Our next goal was to cross the sea highway going through the Straits of Gibraltar, which connects the Atlantic Ocean with the Mediterranean Sea, without being smashed by some big ship. This had happened to Ralph, whose rowing boat was caught under the hull of an enormous tanker in the Indian Ocean. He'd noticed the vessel when it was only 300 metres from him – too late to avoid a collision. The tanker sucked the boat along with Ralph, who'd been shut up in the cabin for quite a long time, underneath it several times. As luck would have it, the boat scraped free just before it was crushed by the tanker's huge propeller and Ralph escaped with just some broken ribs and a broken finger.

To avoid similar crashes, we depended on:

1. The AIS system for automatic identification, which was installed not just on our boat, but almost on all big ships. It alerts sea vessels on course for collision with one another, even before they are several nautical miles away from each other;

2. The radars which nearly all big ships have at their disposal and our passive radar reflector, which has to be detected by them at a distance of several miles. The latter consists of a plastic cylinder filled with broken metal scraps. For increased safety we'd taken a reflector with 20 rather than 10 square metres of metal, which most small yachts and rowing boats used;

3. Our navigation lamp with white, green and red light, as used by yachts;

4. The VHF radio on which we could hail an approaching boat, if nothing else works;

5. A horn with which we would give a sound signal, especially in fog; it could be heard on a sailing yacht but would hardly be heard on a big ship.

About 300 ships a day pass through the Gibraltar Straits and although we were passing about 200 nautical miles from the straits, over the course of a few days, we kept seeing several big ships around us at the same time. We followed these vessels on the chartplotter and tracked whether they were heading in our direction.

One of these huge ships, which was approaching us from the horizon, was moving very strangely, its prow pointed at us for a minute, then pointed elsewhere. It had clearly noticed us through the AIS system, because they called us on the radio, addressing us by the name of our boat, NEVEREST, to tell us that their engine had broken down and their ship was drifting uncontrollably in the ocean. We confirmed that we'd received the warning, and we'd take care not to come close. We continued on our course, passing the drifting ship by more than two nautical miles.

Rather more stressful, was our encounter with a big fishing boat, which was on a collision course with us at a speed of 13 knots. It approached terrifyingly quickly and though I began to row with all my strength to get out of its way, it was as if its prow was deliberately pointing at us – like the muzzle of a canon, from which any moment a cannonball would fly and wipe out its target. We saw the name of the boat on the AIS system and called it up on the radio, but didn't get a reply. We called a second time – again nothing. Only at the third call the watchman on duty answered that they'd seen us and the boat suddenly changed course by 90 degrees, when we were less than one nautical mile from each other. After it distanced itself by about two nautical miles, it stopped and remained in one place for quite a long time. This behaviour seemed quite strange and unexplainable to us – perhaps it was simply searching for schools of fish.

Chapter 16

DARK NIGHTS
18-20 JUNE 2020, MAX

Already in the first days on the ocean, rowing conditions became much more extreme than during our training sessions on the Black and Aegean seas. We'd read in meteorological books that the size of waves in the ocean depended on the speed of the wind, its duration and fetch – the distance over water that the wind blows in a single direction. During our voyage we realised this was entirely true; when the wind speed increased, the height of the waves increased; they became ever steeper, and the peaks of some of them began to foam and break. During the day we managed to keep the boat under control – i.e. we were travelling on our chosen course and avoided leaving the boat side on to the waves, so they didn't capsize us.

Rowing on the ocean is a lot more dynamic and varied than in calm waters. The rise and fall of the waves means that the two oars don't make contact with the water simultaneously. With almost every oar stroke, the oar blades penetrate the water at different depths and so meet different resistance. Sometimes, one oar simply doesn't enter the water. Another time, one oar unexpectedly hits the peak of a wave and its handle bashes painfully into your thigh or kneecap. I've been hit this way on a number of occasions, sometimes it doesn't hurt, but other times my leg has been throbbing for a long time after the knock. All of this leads to different strains on the arms with every oar stroke. When a foaming wave appears, the rower has to react quickly, speeding up or slowing down his rowing, so as not to allow it to turn or capsize the boat.

It was a lot more unpleasant and dangerous when the waves came from the side of the boat. Then NEVEREST rocked wildly to the left and right and the oars stabbed like knives into the water. This put both us and the oars at risk. Also, if the blade of the oar happened to be turned parallel to the water and slapped over it, the oar handle would bash into the rower's leg and bruise it black and blue. Usually these blows would be followed by an "ow" or "ouch"!

Rowing amongst waves was a constant challenge, even in the daytime. During subsequent nights however, neither the moon nor the stars could be seen and around our boat it was as dark as in a cave. The lamp over the cabin lit the water only several metres from the boat, but as we inched across the water's surface, its light dissipated into the surroundings and only a minimal fraction returned to our eyes. This hampered our advance warning of oncoming waves. We saw them only just before they unleashed an attack on us.

The noise of these breaking waves during the night was petrifying. It created a vision of an avalanche which any second would swallow the boat. You could hear them break, not just on deck, but in the cabin where the walls were thinner than two centimetres and the sound of the ocean resonated within. When the crest of the waves swallowed NEVEREST, the whole boat tossed about and vibrated and sometimes woke up whoever was sleeping in the cabin, as if he'd been woken by an earthquake. My father continually tried to distinguish normal sounds from those that might indicate a fracture or some other damage to the boat, and he wouldn't rest until he was sure that everything was in order.

While we rowed we had to be continuously alert, so that we could correct the course of the boat as quickly as possible or at the very least, remain on the sliding seat when some wave washed over us; of course we didn't always succeed, and sometimes we ended up sprawled across the deck. With one such tumble out of the seat, I dropped one of the oars. It thrust into the water, twisted and broke the oarlock that held it, even bending the 10-millimetre metal pin, which it turned on. Luckily, the oar did not break or get lost in the waves. In a minute we'd cast the Jordan anchor and got busy changing the oarlock and its pin. We expected such incidents, which is why we'd taken six spare oarlocks and two spare pins. It was like changing a tyre in a car race. We wanted to finish as quickly as possible and continue with our rowing.

When another big wave flooded the boat, and filled it to its oarlocks, the water swept one of the 10-litre drinking water containers and a thermos overboard. As we'd made 20 drain-holes, the boat emptied in seconds, however, after that we began to tie down all items on the deck – bottles for drinking and urinating, the bucket for washing clothes and for the toilet, the drinking water containers, shoes for rowing and all clothes and socks which were drying on lines. The two drogues and the life-raft were already tied fast to the deck from the start of the voyage, so we didn't lose them if the boat capsized.

The feeling of rowing at night was scary and exhilarating at the same time – like a new sport which requires you to be aware of the danger to your life while mastering the technique of the exercise. During the first days on the ocean I began practising rowing during the day with my eyes closed – by feeling instead of seeing. I learnt to sense where the wind was blowing from by its touch on my face and my ears, and to better discern the direction from which the waves were coming, although often they reached us from different sides. With the boat rocking in the waves, the oars entered and left the water at different times, every stroke was different from the previous one. I had to get used to not reel too much when a wave suddenly crashed into the blade of my oar or when I was just rowing thin air.

UFO?
17 JUNE 2020, STEFAN

One night we witnessed a phenomenon we'd never seen before – an Unidentified Flying Object (UFO), similar to a long string of white Christmas lights or a flying train with brightly lit windows, but pointing straight up, almost vertically towards the sky. It seemed the UFO was not moving but was frozen in the vault-like ceiling of the sky. The intensity of its lights didn't change and it was strong enough for me to catch it with the camera on my mobile phone. I don't think the object was a meteorite because it was not falling headlong down and it didn't look like a head with a tail, instead all its lights were equally bright. Neither was it a plane or a ship.

Apart from the line of lights close to the surface of the water, there was an even bigger and brighter light above. Was this the base from which the UFO had flown? Its light was so strong that from it to the boat, it was reflected in the water like a lunar path. We could not work out how far away it was from us, or how big the shining objects were, because in the dark we had nothing to orient ourselves with. After standing motionless in the sky for quite a while, the rosary of lights and the other strong light hid behind clouds and disappeared. We had expected to see ships, sharks, waves and goodness knows what else, but not a UFO over the ocean!

THE BIG WAVES
21-23 MAY 2020, MAX

About a week after setting out, the wind began to grow stronger and stronger, and the waves became bigger and more terrifying. Ralph had warned us that between Portugal and the Canary Islands, we'd probably encounter big waves. He told us that in this region his boat was capsized by a wave, not sideways, as it happened most of the time, but lengthwise. The stern was lifted so high by the wave that it turned over the prow and the boat had fallen down so hard on the water surface that the sliding seat broke away. Without the sliding seat, ocean rowing is exceptionally ineffective and Ralph was forced to send out an SOS. He was lucky that this happened only a day after leaving Portugal and a Portuguese warship managed to save not just him, but his boat as well. In rescue operations, usually only the crew are saved and their boats are left to the ocean until they are cast on some shore. This is the reason that it's recommended to have a tracker with a charged battery that can send a location signal via satellite for months. It's also a good idea to leave a note with the telephone number and email of the owner, in the event of the boat being found by some honourable person. We'd taken these precautions before starting our voyage.

For several days in a row, the wind speed exceeded 20 knots and its direction was pretty much constant from the north-northeast; the fetch started to surpass 150-200 nautical miles, so the average height of the waves began to exceed 3 metres. This meant that every several minutes waves came about, two times taller than the average – 6 metres, and from time to time, three times as tall – about 9 metres. We began to worry about how things would develop from then on.

The ocean waves were mighty, juddering, unique and magnificent. They stacked on top of each other, in layers – waves over waves, over waves... At the very base were the huge swells, hundreds of metres long that slowly, slowly rose and fell, and which I'd never seen the like of in the seas. Over these, in a greater hurry, wave-hills were chasing, running one after the other or colliding, coming from different directions. Then on the third layer, waves of whirling water foamed up here and there and applied the final touches to the landscape. In the raging waters I discovered an indescribable beauty and for hours I gazed at the wave commotion, never tiring of it for a second.

Was it terrifying? Yes. It was terrifying to not know from which side the next wave would engulf you, to expect every minute that a wave might capsize you and you'd end up being trapped under the boat or swept too far away from it to have a chance of reaching it. It was terrifying, and there was a serious risk of capsizing as the wind got stronger and the waves got higher and higher – we didn't know how wild the elements would become and how the boat would endure them.

The fact that my whole family were passionate about snowboarding and we loved to spend time in the mountains, helped me adapt to the big waves in the ocean. For snowboarders, a 5 to 10-metre hill is not at all scary. The mountain pistes sweep down hundreds of metres. So I imagined that the boat merged with my body like a snowboard and together we slid down the hills.

We'd asked some ocean rowers at what wave height or at what wind speed it would be sensible to stop rowing and cast the drogue. One adventurer answered that her land based team insisted she stopped rowing when the wind speed exceeded 18 knots. All the others said that they'd never had strictly predetermined limits – everything depended on the particular conditions, like how steep the waves were, whether they were breaking at the top, whether they were coming from one or multiple directions and to what extent the rowers themselves felt confident they could manage. The design and size of the boat were also important, as the bigger seagoing vessels were usually more stable than the smaller ones. We didn't, therefore, keep to strict rules for casting the anchor; we did it when the boat began to become unmanageable amidst huge waves or when the headwinds or side winds were so strong as to make struggling against them futile.

NO TEARS ON BOARD
STEFAN

Max and I had read books by ocean rowers and watched documentaries about narrow escapes on rowing boats in the oceans. These people had experienced the adventure of their lives and had witnessed countless unique dawns and sunsets, encountered beautiful bizarre sea creatures and experienced spiritual peace and fulfilment. All of them had inevitably run up against huge waves, communication and navigational instrument failures, total exhaustion, loneliness, panic, pain, encounters with sharks, fear of the worst and goodness knows what else. One of these documentary films followed the crossing of the Atlantic by two big strong men; they were often filmed with tears and snot streaming down their faces, even though they were in front of the camera. Then again, other rowers joked about their vicissitudes. Max and I had decided that we would try to overcome the difficulties with humour, rather than tears.

Before setting out on our voyage, Max's aunt Dessi Schachne, advised us to view the events on our voyage as though they were neutral in colour and to paint them in whatever colours we ourselves chose. She talked to us of how adversities like headwinds, storms, the hot sun and other phenomena around us are not there to deliberately break us, and therefore we should enjoy them instead of cursing them. This entirely resonated with my sense of the world – that you alone choose the attitude and the lens to view the things that happen around you. I remembered how when a busker got on the metro, some passengers smiled and gave him the odd coin, others frowned and even changed carriage, and still others acted as though they hadn't noticed his presence. Looked at objectively, the busker himself had neither a positive nor a negative effect on people around him, every person chose for themselves how to react to him.

I've felt the positive influence of this attitude of overcoming obstacles during mountain marathons as well. When you know that there are still 100 kilometres left to the finish and feel that you haven't the strength for a tenth of them, it really helps to focus on positive thoughts. Enjoy the beautiful natural sights around you, breathe in the smell of the pine trees, tell yourself that what lies ahead of you can be achieved, etc., rather than concentrating on the parts of the body that are hurting, looking for a rational explanation for why you weren't fully prepared or simply feeling sorry for yourself.

Chapter 17

WATER IN THE BOAT
17-26 JULY 2020, MAX

After we'd spent a few days on the ocean, we noticed that the boat began to get heavier – we were sinking ever lower in the water and moving slower and slower. We reasoned that somewhere, water was leaking in and it turned out we were right. Five of the small holds under the deck were completely flooded. The food packets stored within were floating in pools of water – it was just as well that the lyophilized portions, the bars, nuts, dried fruit, in fact almost all of our food, had been vacuum packed in individual waterproof packets. The tens of hours of work by Jenny and Lara were clearly worth it, going through three shrink-wrap machines (the first two broke down) while they packed the food and some items of the expedition equipment.

We began to pump out the water with a hand pump. This was located on the inside wall of the cabin, and we fastened to it a long hose, with which we were able to access every hold. One of us opened each flooded hold and held the end of the hose close to the bottom, while the other worked the pump, pushing its handle up-and-down with one or two hands. It was a beastly, exhausting exercise, especially when you took into account that apart from this task, each of us was rowing 12 hours a day. The waves continually washed over the deck however, and in the following days these five holds continued to take in about 100 litres of water a day. It was for this reason exactly that we'd built the boat with 13 separate waterproof compartments. The remaining eight, including the cabin, had not collected much water, with the exception of a small quantity from condensation.

We felt the weight of the flooded holds while we rowed, it was as though we were pulling a trailer behind the boat; it wasn't great to row in this way or to pump out the water every day. We discovered that the basic problem was the silicone with which we'd sealed the hatches, although it was designed for use on yachts, clearly it was not a quality product because it split and crumbled and between the deck and the hatch, cracks appeared through which water was able to penetrate. It meant that we were likely going to have to stop in the Canary Islands, take off the hatches that were letting in water and seal them with a more suitable polymer.

PROBLEM WITH THE AUTOPILOT
19-26 JUNE 2020, STEFAN

The autopilot managed the direction of the rudder and hence the direction of movement of the boat 24 hours a day and helped us keep to a less crooked trajectory. This was really helpful. After the second day we did not see land and therefore, had no stationary orientation. The sun, the moon, the stars and the clouds were not visible all of the time and when they did appear, they were never motionless. We could keep a comparatively straight course by using the compass and the instrument showing our coordinates and direction of movement, but without the autopilot, we had to row more often with just one or the other oar to correct the direction of travel.

For us though, the autopilot had an even more useful function: when a wave turned the boat sideways, it helped the rower to return the boat more quickly to the desired direction.

On only the fifth or sixth day into our voyage however, the autopilot began to play up. It started happening two or three times a day but gradually became more and more frequent. Sometimes, a simple reset from the control head, situated next to the rowers seat, was sufficient to reboot it and get it working again. At other times though, it needed to be restarted in the control box situated in the cabin. This required the assistance of the other person, which would interrupt their vital rest period, day and night. This whole process took some time during which the rudder could remain in an unfavourable position and knock us off course or send us into waves that may capsize us. We discussed the problem with Jordan and Pavel Mihaylov from Shiptechnics in Varna on the satellite telephone and following their instructions, we made various tests of the electrical system and the devices with the help of a multimetre. Finally, we concluded that the problem of it cutting out was in the autopilot control head, installed by the rower's seat. They offered to send us a new control head as well as a wireless remote control device for managing the autopilot. Due to these problems with the autopilot, we decided to plot a course to the Canary Islands where we'd stop and repair the boat. We expected to arrive there in a matter of days.

Chapter 18

PIRATES?
21 JULY 2020, MAX

Conditions continued to be comparatively favourable, despite the waves being bigger and the wind stronger than one might wish. It was the middle of the night, the waves were tossing me left and right and were continually pouring over me. I had to concentrate hard the whole time which didn't offer me a moment's rest. I couldn't wait for my shift to finish so I could retreat to the cabin for a sweet nap.

The time for the changeover came, my father left the cabin and I hid inside. I asked if he'd seen anything unusual on the chartplotter and he told me everything was normal. I got undressed, lay down and took one last look at the screen. To my amazement, I saw two approaching sea vessels, heading towards us. I jumped up and looked more carefully. I saw they were coming from the African coast and they were about 4 nautical miles away. One was coming from the northeast and the other from the southeast.

After that I saw that the chartplotter hadn't identified their names, but just their MMSI codes. It was unusual but not impossible. I told myself they were sure to be merchant vessels but just before I went to sleep, both boats disappeared from the chartplotter simultaneously. This was really strange and it was then that I remembered that the previous day Nikolay Djambazov had warned us of the danger of pirates close to the Moroccan shore, because he had had such an encounter himself. I opened the hatch and looked outside, searching for the vessels' lights between the big waves, most of which were a lot taller than our boat. At last I saw them, maybe less than 3 nautical miles from us. We had to hide, because I was convinced that they were indeed pirates. I switched off NEVEREST's AIS system, so they could not see our location on their chartplotters, and after that I asked my father to row in the dark, because I wanted to turn off the lights. He didn't agree easily, because he felt more confident when he could see at least for a few metres around the boat, but even so he still obliged. I was convinced that if we turned off the lights, there would be no way they could find us in the dark and huge waves. NEVEREST was too small and the white foam on the big waves hid our location almost completely. I breathed out, relaxed but was still impatient to find out the situation when I woke. Thankfully, we didn't see them again.

THE BATTLE FOR LANZAROTE
25-26 JULY 2020, STEFAN

We decided to stop in Lanzarote – the easternmost of the Canary Islands, in order to seal the leaks in our provision holds and to fix the faulty autopilot. At first this seemed a sensible decision, we didn't however, expect that it would turn out to be so difficult to achieve.

There was a strong north wind blowing and we were northeast of the island. We had to row to the west – perpendicular to the wind and the waves which were continually flowing over us, tossing and twisting the boat uncontrollably. We were moving in a way that meant we were on the brink of capsizing, but if we didn't keep this course, we would miss the island. We rowed with all our strength. It became impossible to last out two-hour shifts on the oars and so we began to change over every hour. Later – every half hour. The outline and lights of Lanzarote appeared on the horizon. Night fell.

As I rowed through the night, I felt like I was crossing a motorway with my eyes closed, expecting any moment to be run over by a lorry. The island's lights scarcely twinkled ahead of us. On the chartplotter we saw that although the boat's prow was pointing at the island, the boat was moving sideways rather than straight ahead towards it – for every mile to the west, we travelled almost two to the south. It seemed as if we'd overshoot Lanzarote. The struggle continued right through to the end of the night, until we finally managed to reach the island's southeastern coast. We went round it and managed to take shelter in its lee to the south.

I took a breather, at last it seemed to us that we'd reach Lanzarote's marina, which lay a few miles to the west. I even put out some music through the boat's speakers to celebrate, while Max slept on, dead to the world in the cabin before his rowing shift.

We were approaching the harbour, tired but happy, when a wind blew up from the shore, as if from nowhere and strengthened quickly. At this point the boat was positioned between the red and green buoys at the entrance of the marina itself and at this precise moment, the big harbour tug bearing the PILOT inscription, approached us. This tug managed the ships' berthing and it warned us through a loud hailer, that we should draw back from the fairway because a big container ship was going to enter the harbour. We had already noticed the big ship approaching from a few miles away and in a matter of minutes, it was at the harbour entrance. We had to turn the boat and slip down with the wind, distancing ourselves from the yacht marina. The ship passed and we tried to return to the harbour, but it became harder and harder to make progress.

We were at the end of our strength. We were changing over the rowing every five or ten minutes. We didn't want to seek help, but we soon realised that instead of moving into the marina channel, we were in fact, getting further and further away and rapidly approaching the rocks to the southwest. We tried to call the pilot tug on the radio, but they passed us over to the marina administration. The dispatcher directed us to radio channel 07 on which to contact the harbour rescue boat. Radio channel 07 did not reply. We sought the marina and the pilot tug again. Finally, the pilot boat which had driven us away from the marina entrance returned and threw us a rope, pulling us several hundred metres inside the harbour breakwater. We couldn't believe it, but minutes after that we were stepping onto dry land in Lanzarote!

A STOP FOR REPAIRS
26 JUNE - 5 JULY 2020, MAX

A few days before reaching Lanzarote we had agreed with the Shiptechnics team that they would send two new autopilot control devices to the island marina. They had duly sent them off by courier with the hope that the parts would get to the island before us. The dispatch however, was delayed by customs officials, the situation with coronavirus and the Canary Islands' bureaucratic procedures. We had to liaise with the couriers every day as the package travelled from Bulgaria via Spain and Tenerife and finally arrived in Lanzarote a week late. It took us less than an hour to install the device, but it turned out that the battery of the wireless remote control didn't work despite being brand new. We had no choice but to change the device from being 'wireless' to 'wired up', by connecting it up with cables to the boat's electrical system. Thus, we now had two separate new devices with which to manage the autopilot.

Meanwhile, before our arrival to the island, my mother had already begun to look for new round hatches like those on our boat, so we could exchange them if we broke any of the original ones when fixing the leaks to the hold. A friend of a friend – Yana Sotirova, who lived in Lanzarote, had rushed to assist and had done the rounds of every one of the island's boating spare-part shops with her car and had found some that sold similar hatches. On the very day of our arrival, Yana bundled us into her car and took us shopping but sadly it turned out that none of the hatches available were the right size. The staff in these shops were certain that if they ordered the size of hatches we needed, they would arrive in two to four weeks time. Given this was not a viable option for us, with the greatest possible care, we set about unsticking the foundations of the five hatches that were leaking water, so as not to break them, and after two days we managed to remove them, clean them of the old silicone and re-stick them with polymer that we had purchased locally following recommendations. Just in case, we took off the remaining two round hatches in the deck and stuck them down again and lastly we applied this polymer round the frames of the four rectangular hatches on the boat without taking them off.

By this point in our voyage we had both lost a few kilos in weight, so after 12 days of rowing, we set about restoring this while on the island. My father and I ate as if we were four people – morning, noon and night. We mostly chose restaurants with Italian or Chinese cuisines and we'd each order two main meals. The tastiest thing that I ate on the island was a combination of pizza and pasta. I grabbed the pizza like a pitta bread and spread a sizable amount of pasta on it – the result was something like an Italian taco. I'm sure it sounds horrible, but that's exactly what I craved. The waiting staff often warned us we were ordering too much food, but we managed to consume not only the main meals but a dessert or two as well!

We made use of our time on land to get some decent rest and slept for 10 or 12 hours a day, working on the boat the rest of the time. We were so fortunate to have Yana to help us and show us around Lanzarote. The island was almost completely deserted because of the coronavirus pandemic and although it had been officially open for tourists in the last few days, there weren't any. There had only been one case of Covid on the island up to this point, a foreigner who'd been treated and had returned to his country. Despite this, everybody wore masks on the streets and were of the opinion that they'd have to get used to them so as to be ready for the return of tourists, without whom the island could not survive economically.

Yana took us to some picturesque bays and her favourite restaurants, as well as the incredible Timanfaya National Park, which looked like a volcanic island where a few years earlier, a volcano had erupted and where plants have still not managed to regrow. In some of the crevasses a few metres below the surface, the temperature reaches 400 degrees Celsius and if someone were to throw a bucket of water down it, it would immediately erupt into steam like a geyser. The only restaurant in the park serves meat grilled over the heat emitted from the bowels of the earth.

Yana was an exceptionally interesting person. She was one of Bulgaria's 'Golden Girls' – a World and European Rhythmic Gymnastics champion, from Neshka Robeva's team. After that she worked in the legendary Cirque du Soleil and later circled the oceans on big cruise ships. When we were introduced to her in Lanzarote, she was teaching rhythmic gymnastics to little children. She told us that when she was young, she'd trained for the Bulgarian national team from dawn to dusk. They had to repeat every exercise ten times without a mistake before they could go to bed. They weren't even given enough water to drink and often had to resort to taking water from flower vases and even toilet cisterns to quench their thirst. At breakfast they were allowed to eat one spoon of honey with half a walnut, at lunch a piece of melted cheese and at supper half an apple or kiwi, and only provided they kept to the weight norm. Considering these training sessions and diet in mind, ocean rowing seemed like a doddle to us.

Although we were burning with impatience to continue with our voyage, we had to wait for a couple of days for the storm winds to die down around the island before we could set off.

Chapter 19

AT THE QUARTER MARK OF OUR JOURNEY TO BRAZIL
9 JULY 2020, STEFAN

After we set off from Lanzarote, we had to be careful the wind didn't blow us onto the rocks of Fuerteventura Island. You'll not be surprised to hear that yet again we had to struggle with the wind – this time we were forced to row across it, with the boat's prow to the southeast, while it was coming from the northeast. After we'd passed the island we had to change direction to the southwest, so as not to be wrecked on African shores. Before Lanzarote, we had almost rubbed noses with potential pirates at about 70 nautical miles from the Moroccan coast, and after leaving the island the wind had brought us to 35 nautical miles from Morocco. Luckily, no more pirates turned up as we gradually began to distance ourselves once again from the shoreline, heading southwest on the ocean.

On the 16th day on water, we passed the 800th nautical mile (1500th kilometre) with which we marked what was pretty much a quarter of our planned voyage to Brazil. This gave us hope and confidence that we could succeed in reaching the end.

The previous day, we'd rowed in winds of 20 to 22 knots and amidst 'washing machine waves'. When we lived in Brazil, that's what the local surfers called the waves coming at you from all sides – with no aim or direction. We managed through the day, although from time to time the waves crashed over our deck but during the night, we cast the drogue and shut ourselves in the cabin.

That night was long and almost sleepless as the waves relentlessly bashed the boat from all sides. We had to keep the hatch closed so water didn't get into the cabin, and therefore, the inside became exceptionally hot and airless. We were drenched in sweat and woke every hour from the boat's rocking motion and the suffocating space. We opened the hatch for a few seconds, enough for some fresh air to enter, and closed it again before a deluge of waves engulfed us.

In the morning we discovered that the rope for retrieving the anchor had become untied. This was not the thick main rope with which the anchor was tied to the prow, but the thin floating rope, tied to the top of the parachute, which made it easier for us to retrieve the floating anchor. So once again we had to haul in by hand, the 80-metre long rope, along with the open parachute. This time it had not fallen under the boat, but the winds were exceeding 20 knots and the waves were two to three metres high.

Throughout the whole night, the winds blew from the northeast and, because of the strong current, we had travelled back about 7 nautical miles

(13 kilometres) in that direction. The next day, we had to row it again. This current was the reason we were moving more slowly than expected, but soon we tore ourselves out of its clutches and things fell into place.

Chapter 20

THE BEAUTY OF THE OCEAN
8 JULY 2020, MAX

Solitary voyages on the ocean offer seafarers incredible views and experiences which cannot be seen or felt from dry land and which will never be forgotten. This happened during our voyage too, experiencing magical nights when we had the luck to row through streams of bioluminescent plankton. The sight of thousands of tiny shining plankton drifting alongside our boat, reminded me of a meadow lit up with millions of dancing fireflies. With every movement of water around our boat, their glow increased, as though their dance was quickening. Globes of blue fire formed around the oar blades and behind us we left a long shining trail in our wake. In the cloudless nights when the sky and the sea merged, the rowing through the plankton's sparkle made me feel as though I was piloting a spacecraft, surrounded by a million stars. Since Interstellar is one of my favourite films, this unforgettable sight was even dearer to me! The ocean turned out to be a lot more than I'd imagined.

FIRST SEA FISHING
10 JULY 2020, STEFAN

Following the advice of the ocean fisherman Kolio Bo-zakov (Kole Kole), we fastened a rubber hose to one of the cleats, and to that, a 15-metre line at the end of which, we tied a feather with two hooks and a colour-ed metal fish lure. The rubber hose was necessary so the line wouldn't break if a big fish was caught on the hooks. In the first weeks of rowing, we were too busy with our survival, to think of fishing for food. In any case, we weren't quite managing with the daily food portions which Jenny and Lara had prepared for us. We were only able to consume, on average, three quarters of our daily rations of around 4650 calories, which meant that we were taking in about 3500 cal-ories a day only. We were probably expending over 5000 calories a day, in other words, we were accu-mulating an energy deficit of at least 1500-2000 cal-ories a day. Quite naturally therefore, we were losing body mass every day. On top of this, we were burning off not just fat, but also muscle that was not actively employed in the exercise of rowing.

So, on the third week, we cast our line for the first time at about 100 nautical miles to the south of the Canary Islands. We left the lure to be dragged in our wake as we rowed. We hadn't tied it properly though and it jumped over the surface of the water. On a sec-ond casting, when the lure had sunk below the wa-ter's surface, we had beginner's luck and caught our first fish – a little over two feet long. We weren't sure what it was, but it looked like a mahi-mahi.

Kole had explained to me how to fillet a fish, so we could eat it raw as sashimi. There was only one, not especially sharp knife, left on board as the others had rusted to such an extent that they could not be used. One way or another however, I managed to carve a fillet from the fish, get rid of the skin and chop it into thin strips. Max and I really loved sashimi, but had only tried salmon and tuna. Jenny had put a bottle of soy sauce into our food luggage, so that we were able to make it into a real feast and ate the whole fish in one go. We only lacked wasabi.

To be honest, the sashimi from this fish was not as tender as salmon, but perhaps the fault lay with us, we didn't react quickly enough to kill it once it landed on deck. It may have thrashed around too long while I tried to reach it and end its suffering with the first thing I managed to grab – the big drinking water container.

FLYING FISH AND DANGEROUS SEA PREDATORS
10 JULY 2020, MAX

The night after our first fishing session, flying fish appeared. Until this point in time, neither of us had seen such fish but it turned out they do actually exist. They began to bombard our boat over the following days and nights. They were between 10 and 30 centimetres long and had side fins, a little shorter than their bodies. The fins looked like bat's wings and allowed them to fly at dizzying speed above the water's surface. They usually flew 10 to 20 metres, before diving again into the water, but we've also seen them fly longer distances. At night time the lamp above the cabin attracted them and they shot at us like bullets, often crashing into the boat and falling onto the deck where they thrashed for less than a minute, before dying. Sometimes they appeared suddenly and hit the rower's face, chest or arms leaving a strong fishy smell. Once, one of them actually flew into the cabin, while my father was sleeping in there. The smell spread throughout the whole space, while he tried to catch it and throw it back into the water. From that moment on we began to keep the hatch pretty much closed, even on the calmest nights.

We joked that a flying fish could leap by itself into the pot on the gas cooker and one night it really happened. A flying fish, about a foot long, in its unsuccessful effort to fly over the boat, fell directly into the pot which was fastened next to the big hatch behind the rower. As neither my father nor I had seen it, it sadly died inside the pot. It was too small to feed us so we threw it back into the sea. In the beginning, when flying fish fell on the boat, we stopped rowing and jumped to save them before they died. Then we realised that in the water around us, bigger fish were lying in wait for exactly this opportunity and would gobble them up the moment they fell back into the water. As our rescue operations turned out to be pointless, we stopped breaking our rowing rhythm every time a fish landed on deck and subsequently, the next day would often find five to ten dead fish on our deck which we returned to the sea before NEVEREST began to smell like a fishing boat!

Soon, there formed around us, a shoal of bigger fish, between half to one metre long, mostly mahi-mahi, in bright, phosphorescent blue, green, yellow, or silver colours. There were others – black, grey or brown fish. Clearly, they had all been attracted by the flying fish which they liked to eat. The shoal began to travel alongside us day and night for weeks, sometimes there were 5 to 10 fish, other times, 30 to 40. The moment a flying fish hit the boat and fell into the water, the surface began to boil from the large fishes' race to the prey. If we threw out a bit of food, the same thing happened. Sometimes as I washed the utensils over the side of the boat, some fish would bite on the spoon or my finger, making it bleed. When these predatory fish gathered around us for the first time, I thought that if we jumped in the water to clean the boat or to cool down, they'd attack us and pick us clean like piranhas, but this didn't happen. Clearly, size mattered – they were bold enough to bite my finger, but when I jumped in the water amongst them, they swam around without attacking me.

Mahi-mahi were clearly the favourite food for even bigger predatory fish though – sharks, swordfish, marlin, etc. Sometimes in the distance we saw how one-metre long mahi-mahis leapt like flying fish over the water in a sequence of five or six leaps, chased by huge fish, several metres long. This activity foamed up the water to such an extent, that you heard the roar hundreds of metres away. The rumbling it created reminded me of big hammer drills breaking up concrete. Often the mahi-mahi would aim straight for NEVEREST, chased by some bigger monster, which once it sensed the presence of the boat, would dive into the depths and not appear again. Perhaps that was another reason for them congregating around our boat.

Now that there were so many fish gathered around NEVEREST, fishing for food became pretty easy. Sometimes I just threw a line with a hook into the water and the black fish, which seemed to be the hungriest, got caught on it. Mahi-mahi were a little more intelligent and to catch them we had to put on a flying fish as bait, but if it had been on deck for more than a few hours, they didn't touch it. The bait had to be fresh and then it only took seconds or minutes to catch a mahi-mahi, especially at night time.

And I too gained the skill of filleting the fish and preparing sashimi. The mahi-mahi was such a big fish that we could not eat all of it raw in one go. First we made sashimi for breakfast or lunch and for the next meal we boiled up a fish soup on the gas cooker with a few spoons of bouillon. Thus, one fish took the place of the lyophilized food for a whole day – we were forced to save on this crucial food resource as it looked to us like the voyage would take longer than we'd initially planned.

One time, when we were moored on the drogue because of a strong headwind, my father tried to grab by hand one of the grey scaled fish, which was swimming slowly round the boat. It was too slippery however, and it slid out of his hands. Then he decided to try with a knife, and with a quick stroke, he stabbed it and threw it straight on to the deck. It turned out to be pretty good for sashimi and fish soup – skinning it was trickier though because of the large scales.

A few days later I managed to stab such a fish with a knife as well. This motivated me to fashion a spear from the tiller, at the end of which I tied some rope and wrapped our sharp knife with duck-tape. I tried diving and catching fish with it, but my movements in the water were pretty slow and I couldn't catch anything. Fishing with a spear from the deck of the boat didn't work either. So we continued traditional angling with bait and hook, which worked without fail. There were so many mahi-mahi, which are in some parts or the world considered a real delicacy, that there was no reason to switch to trying to catch other fish. Mahi-mahi are exceptionally tender and tasty, especially when we managed to put them out of their misery with a swift hammer blow to the head.

Only once did we boil a soup from the biggest flying fish we found on the deck – it was about 35 centimetres long. It was edible, but had quite a lot of bones and was not especially tasty. During the entire voyage, we managed to catch twelve big fish – nine mahi-mahi, two grey scaled fish and one – a kind not known to us.

SHARKS
STEFAN

Naturally, we encountered sharks. I remember during one of our evenings in Portugal, in answer to Jenny's question, our friend and navigator, Ralph Tuijn told us that sharks seldom attack ocean rowing boats. He'd encountered lots of sharks during his voyages across the Atlantic, Pacific and Indian Oceans. Only one incident with a shark had befallen him and that was not far from where we were in the Atlantic. A shark had bitten off his whole rudder and he and the remaining five rowers were forced to turn the boat, stern forward and row in this way for more than 1000 nautical miles.

The first time we saw a shark, we decided to christen it Victoria – from the awe we felt for our trainer Victoria and in order to be more confident that it wasn't going to eat us. Victoria was 2-3 metres long, maybe 4, at most 5, but not longer than 6. In the beginning she made some circuits around NEVEREST in a clockwise direction; then another few anti-clockwise, before losing interest. Clearly she did not know what to do with our boat and disappeared.

The most savage shark we encountered was a Hammerhead – named because of its laterally flattened, elongated head, resembling a hammer. For some reason, it had gone crazy and was turning wildly in the water in small circles – like a dog chasing its tail. It was only a dozen metres from the boat and the water around it rumbled and boiled until in the end it too got bored and disappeared somewhere in the depths.

A FEELING FOR ANOTHER REALITY
MAX

Sometimes I had the feeling we were on another planet, where the physical laws of the Earth did not apply. The horizon for example, was not always horizontal. Sometimes it looked as if it had been tilted to the left or right and so as I rowed, one oar sank deep in the water and the other hardly touched the surface. Another time, I had the feeling that I was racing down a slope, which was a lot more pleasant than the opposite sensation – that of rowing upwards on something like a watery incline, which also sometimes happened. Maybe the balance of the boat had some influence over the sense of a changing horizon, but I was sure that the boat was balanced perfectly horizontally. Often the horizon, instead of seeming far away and level with my eyes, seemed quite close and somewhere on the top of a hill behind the boat. Then, waves rolled down this hill towards our stern and pushed us ahead. So as I rowed with my face towards the stern, it seemed to me that we were travelling at a wild speed through the waves, which made me row even more enthusiastically and effectively. And when a larger wave reached us and rose up behind the boat, it happened that I was looking eye to eye with some ocean fish – as if I was under water, or as if the fish was flying over the watery surface.

Chapter 21

I wonder why people give their boats female names given that boats grow beards?! The alternative anti-fouling paste which we had applied as a final coat on the hull in order to prevent sea flora and fauna sticking to it, had done its job for the first month on the water. After that however, more and more barnacles were becoming attached to the hull. This was slowing us down.

We had planned to clean the hull at least once a week with several different tools. None of these were specially made for the job, but we'd taken them to experiment – which of them would be the easiest to clean off the marine inhabitants: a car ice scraper; metal and plastic spatulas for applying plaster and putty; old debit cards. It turned out that the ice scraper was the most effective. So as not to lose it in the ocean we tied it to our wrists while we were cleaning the boat.

I must admit that we put off the first cleaning for quite some time – until the rowing began to feel like dragging a coach without wheels. With every passing nautical mile to the south, the sun burned ever stronger and the weather became ever hotter. So now we had two reasons to jump into the water – to clean the hull and to cool down. Of course, I was scared of sharks, my memories of the film Jaws came to mind, but I was reassured by the fact that we'd heard that sharks usually didn't attack prey out of the blue, but swam round them in ever tightening circles. Later, a friend who'd watched popular documentaries on the subject told me that some sharks attacked shooting upwards from the depths, biting their victim and even jumping with them out of the water, where they adjusted them between their teeth.

Even so, we decided it would be safer if one of us stayed on board the boat and looked out for sharks, while the other cleaned the hull. That being said, the person in the water was also prepared to punch the shark in the nose or to stab its eye, which we'd heard sometimes dissuades it from attack. After the first cleaning of the hull in the ocean it seemed to us that the average speed of the boat increased by at least 0.5 knots. This doesn't seem a lot, but spread over time, would gain us about 12 nautical miles (22 kilometres) extra per day.

In the beginning, we cleaned the boat less than once a week and we stayed in the water only for several minutes – enough for one of us to clean one side and the other person, the other side. My technique was to clean 80% of the time under water, and for the remaining 20% to look out for sharks. This strategy gave me the opportunity to learn how to manage the task and help me, little by little, to get used to the idea that there was nothing scary underneath me, and to the feeling that I am more or less helpless in the water. I remember how, during my first two-three dives, my heart began to beat furiously and several stressful scenarios passed through my mind, which was understandable because I was totally inexperienced. I asked my father whether he looked around at all or felt any concern and he assured me that he was careful: he cleaned 98% of the time and looked about for the remaining 2%.

At this stage of the voyage, I found diving into the water quite scary, only later did I realise it wasn't so bad after all. Over time, I gained courage and we jumped into the water almost every day – not only to remove some barnacles or other crustaceans from the hull, but to swim with the fish. Under the boat, schools of fish gathered, mostly sparkling blue mahi-mahi with yellow tails, but also the greatest variety of other types of fish, between a half and one metre in length. Most of them, I thought, had never seen a man swimming so awkwardly among them and they weren't scared of us at all.

FASTER THAN TURTLES
15 JULY 2020, STEFAN

While we were swimming amongst the fish, I realised how clumsy and slow we were. In the boat we were managing to move at 2-2.5 knots (3.7-4.6 kilometres per hour) on average and when the wind was blowing in our direction, scarcely 3-3.5 knots (5.5-6.5 kilometres per hour). The maximum speed which we'd reached was 8.2 knots (15.2 kilometres per hour) and this was only for a few seconds. When some big wave caught up with us, the boat slowed down while climbing to the top and sped up on the way down the wave's back. NEVEREST weighed over a ton and we never managed to surf with her on the face of a single wave. We were so slow that the fish who'd been swimming alongside for weeks, hardly moved their bodies to travel at our speed, and when a flying fish fell into the water, they shot at it from all directions like torpedoes. To our joy, we discovered that we were at least faster than sea turtles. Some of them were intrigued by the boat and when we passed them by, they tried to catch up but with no success. Even with leisurely rowing we managed to outcrawl them.

ENCOUNTER WITH ORCAS
18 JUNE 2020, MAX

It was the latest in a succession of lovely days on the boat – sunny with small wispy clouds which were enough to protect us from the unbearable heat. As I rowed I looked out to the horizon, as I often did. I'd do this most of all to vary my view and to have the time to avoid an accidental collision with some container ship or other sea vessel. But this time it was different – I saw two fins rise up above the water. I immediately thought they were likely to be dolphins, so I calmly knocked on the hatch to wake my father. He got up slowly and leisurely and gave me a look which showed his clear displeasure that I'd woken him up. I told him that a family of dolphins were approaching us, so he should get his camera ready to film them. That was when I asked if there were black dolphins with curved fins and I realised that these were probably not dolphins after all, especially as their fins were suspiciously large. I was filled with joy and a little worry at the same time. I turned back again and began to shout "Orcas! Orcas! Those are orcas, not dolphins." My father hurried to extract his phone from its waterproof cover so he could film better. Looking closely over the water, I wanted to roughly count them. One, two, three fins popped up, then another five and yet five more. I couldn't believe how many and I couldn't fail to notice that every one of them was bigger than the boat. There were 30 to 40 at least and they were moving relatively slowly. I reckoned we were 100 to 150 metres from them and hoped we could get even closer. I changed course and began to row energetically so as to see them closer up.

My father wasn't sure that it was a good idea to row amidst dozens of orcas – he said it was no accident that they were called 'killer whales'. He remembered he'd seen a documentary in which orcas rocked an iceberg to and fro to dislodge a seal, perched upon it in order to eat it. I reassured him that as far as I knew there were no recorded instances of orcas killing a human out in the wild sea, but he wasn't entirely convinced. Well, what if there had been hundreds of such events but no witnesses left to tell the story... Later, a friend of ours sent us a BBC article which, with photographic and video material, told how in this same year – 2020, close to the Spanish and Portuguese coasts from which we'd started our voyage, there had been about 40 incidents in which orcas, weighing 3 to 4 tons had attacked yachts and boats of different sizes. Usually they attacked the rudders, sticking out from under the vessels' hulls. Luckily, the article mentioned that there had been no fatalities and thank goodness, we were left unscathed and our boat untouched.

PORTUGUESE MAN-OF-WAR
18 JULY 2020, STEFAN

After the orcas had moved too far away, Max finally stopped his energetic attempts to catch up with them and furiously stabbed an oar into the water. Right at this spot, a long purple balloon popped up, a little bigger than a fist, from the upper side of which a purple comb protruded, similar to the sail on an ancient boat. It looked like seaweed from which we could make a fresh sea salad. It was just as well that I had become familiar with these sea creatures during my preparation for swimming the English Channel. I hadn't seen them there, but from this moment on, we began to see them nearly every day. These were the Portuguese man-of-war – one of the most poisonous types of jellyfish in the world, whose sting causes suffocation and sometimes a heart attack.

SOMETHING ALWAYS BREAKS DOWN
21 JULY 2020, MAX

If you've read books or seen films about seafarers, it cannot have escaped your notice that something is always breaking down on their vessels and they're always having to repair this or that part. Well, it turns out we were no exception to this rule.

One day, we noticed that the monitors on the two rechargeable batteries registered that their level of charge had fallen to about 60%. This was strange in that up to this moment, they'd been always charged to 80-100% by the solar panels.

We carried out a full check of the electrical system and established that three out of the four solar panels generated a charge of between 0 and 12 volts and accordingly they could in no way recharge the 12 volt batteries. I noticed that around the boxes with cables and diodes on some of the solar panels there was a greenish colouring. When we opened one of them, we saw how some of the cables had oxidised and corroded to complete or almost complete disintegration. The panels were manufactured by a Dutch firm and made for use on yachts so we were really disappointed to learn that they had not withstood the sea moisture.

We took down the only panel still working from the side wall of the boat to check its cables and to our joy we discovered that they were in good condition. We sealed the box with a generous quantity of polymer and the next day we moved the panel to the cabin roof where it would be better exposed to the sun.

We reasoned that we were left with the following alternatives for generating electricity:

1. One sound solar panel which was however, small and could generate a maximum of 50W which meant that with it we could only charge some navigational and communications devices.

2. One quite small foldable 6W solar panel, independent of the boat's electrical system, with which we could charge our telephones only.

3. One or some of the oxidised panels, if we eventually managed to resurrect them – we didn't have great hopes of this.

In the event that all these alternatives failed, we were left with the YB3 Tracker which broadcasted our location every several hours via Iridium satellites and allowed us to exchange short messages with our navigators. Its batteries could last another month or two if we used it very sparingly.

Sadly, the working solar panels were too small to feed the electric watermaker. With it we managed in 20 minutes to produce 12 litres of drinkable water. So we were forced to get the Katadyn 35 mechanical watermaker out of the hold and over the following days we began to filter seawater by hand via a long handle. Because in one hour of non-stop pumping we managed to produce four litres of drinkable water, each of us was forced to add 60 to 90 minutes of work with the watermaker to the 12 hours of rowing per day. Even without this pumping, we only managed five or six hours of sleep per day and we hadn't even got past the halfway point to Brazil. My father and I were on our knees from the rowing and pumping, but we were determined not to give up and seek help from a ship just because of the difficulties with electrical supply.

I tried to regard pumping the mechanical water-maker positively – the movement of the arm was comparable to that in arm wrestling, and certainly if I continued to pump for 60 to 90 minutes every day until the voyage was over, I'd become invincible in this sport... or at least in my school! That's what I told myself, to at least add some amusing stimulus.

Sadly, due to the corrosion of the solar panels, we had to stop using the autopilot and start to control the rudder with ropes. We had planned for this eventuality before setting off. We were able to fasten these ropes in clamps close to our feet so we could keep the rudder stationary at any angle to the stern that we wanted. Every time we needed to change it however, we had to put the oars behind our back and lean forward to rearrange the ropes in the clamps, and then once again retrieve the oars and adjust them in the oarlocks. The whole operation would take seconds and fortunately we wouldn't have to do it very often. Sometimes many hours passed, without our having to even touch the ropes, but I was worried about what we'd do in the night amidst big waves, when the boat is turned sideways. I was worried I'd have to let go of the oars and without accessing any orientation device beyond a scarcely flickering compass at my feet, to change the angle of the rudder exactly when huge waves broke over the boat. It turned out that my fears were worse than the reality. Even in the big waves and strong wind, when the boat turned sideways, it was quite easy to turn it back to the right direction with the manual control of the rudder, while the direction of the wind and the waves served as orientation. After one or two nights' rowing with manual steering, I was even less worried by the boat's unexpected twists and turns because the ropes worked without fail, unlike the autopilot which sometimes cut out at the most critical moments and its restart required switching the electric supply off and on from the panel in the cabin. Sadly, however, in spite of us learning how to manage our navigation without the autopilot, we had to row more often with one oar only, in order to correct the course. This added to our fatigue and made our trajectory a lot more crooked.

So some long days passed by with three defunct solar panels, filtering water by hand, and rowing without the autopilot. A few hundred miles to the south of us lay the Cape Verde Islands and my mother had taken to searching for solar panels there, so we could stop at the westernmost of these islands and replace them. Unluckily, or maybe luckily no solar panels were to be found in Cape Verde, and because of the coronavirus pandemic, flights there were extremely limited and mooring of sea vessels on their shores forbidden. This, of course, didn't put my mother off and she turned the world upside down to find a way to send solar panels from Bulgaria to one of the islands... and a boat to bring them to us, so we didn't have to enter an island harbour. For this to happen however, we'd have had to divert hundreds of nautical miles to the east of our route and get close to the island of Santo Antão, after which we'd set out to the west in pretty unfavourable winds. My father and I therefore decided not to stop in the Cape Verde Islands and to row to the end, even if we didn't manage to fix the three solar panels.

Meanwhile with teeth, nails and creative thinking we got down to fixing the solar panels ourselves on board. The wind and waves rocked the boat endlessly. Two of the solar panels we had to repair were on the roof of the cabin and the aft hold. The hold was easily accessible but to get to the big solar panel cables, my father had to climb over the cabin and to lie with his head down its sloping surface while I held him by the ankles so he didn't fall into the water and tear out some of the antennas for the radio station, satellite telephone and/or the GPS in his path. Even so, we managed to nibble back at the panels' plastic cover over the wires which had corroded, until we got to the healthy wires. Since we didn't have a soldering iron (we'd taken everything in the world except a soldering iron and a vice), we had to think up another way of protecting the wire terminals which were barely reaching the connection with the cables to the rechargeable batteries. We tried gluing rubber caps which would tighten the wires to the cables, but this would not secure the desired connection to the electrical system. We tried screwing plastic caps and this worked with one of the small solar panels. With the biggest and most important one though, this did not work because the screws which we put through the caps, came into contact with some metal tray in the solar panel itself and caused a short circuit. So we were forced to weave the wires we dug out from the solar panel with the electrical system's cables, with the help of metal threads only a little thicker than a hair. To our relief, this worked and the panel returned to life. We had to quickly pour a big amount of polymer over these perilously unprotected wires, in order to cement them in and keep the sea water out, before some wave washed over them. Temporarily, we plastered the connections with thick duck tape, until the polymer dried out and once again we were able to recharge the batteries and use all the devices on board.

We put all our energy into repairing the solar panels as speedily as possible, so we did not miss the Cape Verde Islands, and more importantly before my mother sent some aircraft carrier, along with a whole fleet of submarines and accompanying ships to rescue us against our will. We had successfully secured the electrical situation and we were not forced to stop again.

What a relief – we could once again switch on devices we'd stopped using, like the AIS system, the radio station and the cabin's stereo system with its speakers. We turned up the music to the maximum and had a ball – we might have scared a few fish though! We could also use the electric watermaker, just a shame I wasn't going to improve my arm wrestling skills, as I'd thought. This really was such a relief for us, our land based team, our family, but most of all my mother.

A NORMAL DAY ON NEVEREST
STEFAN

Although there were probably no two identical days on the voyage, the routine part proceeded as follows:

00:00 Max starts the night rowing shift. We change over every two hours. When something disturbs this rhythm – for example, a storm or a repair – we strive to return to the same changeover times, with the idea that we'll find sleeping easier if we go to sleep more or less at the same time. I take off all my clothes and enter the cabin. I do a routine massage with a cylindrical roller on my back and legs. The rocking of the boat hinders the balancing of my body over the roller and like a circus performer, I support myself with my hands on the floor and walls of the cabin, often avoiding scrunching my face or back by a hairsbreadth. I fall into an immediate and blissful sleep following the accumulated exhaustion.

1:45 The alarm clock rings 15 minutes before the beginning of my next shift. I jump up straight away with the thought that Max has now been rowing for almost two hours and I don't want to force him to row one minute extra after the end of his shift.

I put on only shorts and socks as I am trying to stain fewer clothes, and not pile up too much washing. I put on running shoes, grab a few raw bars, dried fruits or nuts and congratulate Max on the successful finale to his shift.

2:00 I start to row either in complete darkness or under a star studded sky and a moon-path. During the night shifts, we usually listen to podcasts of interviews with interesting personalities, audio books or music.

3:40 I wake Max up for the first time. He mutters something, to the effect that he's heard me and he carries on sleeping.

3:50 I wake Max up a second time.

3:55 I wake Max up a third time. Sometimes I have to wake him up four or five times, until he finally jumps up as if stung by a bee and gets ready in a minute. During the night we try to sleep all the time we are not rowing, but when we subtract the time for undressing, hanging of wet clothes, spreading cream on abraded body parts, eating something small, brushing teeth, looking at the chartplotter, getting dressed again, usually the longest sleep is not more than 90 minutes.

6:00 I start the shift when the day is dawning and the sun is shining straight in my eyes. This is my favourite part of the day – it makes me feel that I am living life to the full, while the rest of the world sleeps on.

It turns out however, that with our travel to the west, dawns gradually began to disappear from my shift, because of the change of time zones. That's why we started to change the time on our watches by an hour, which we did quite arbitrarily – literally when it seemed to us that dawn was breaking too late. After several such changes, we forgot how many times we'd adjusted the time and had no idea what time zone we were in and what the time was in Bulgaria.

9:30 We prepare a breakfast fit for a king. Usually this is my job, because I adore breakfasts. We are supposed to take turns, but generally I make the lunches as well. Max prepares the suppers. I eat before 10:00 and Max eats immediately afterwards. We rub on sunscreen at least twice a day.

12:00 I start a new shift on the oars. Max checks the weather forecast, which we download through the satellite hotspot from PredictWind, or the one we get from Valeri. We check the forecast at least twice a day as the wind often changes, especially in the Intertropical Convergence Zone.

14:00 Once a day, when the sun is at its strongest, we put on the watermaker for 10 to 20 minutes to fill the containers with drinkable water. We're constantly hanging wet clothes to dry, and it's best not to mention how rarely we launder them. After the first several weeks, we had to clean the boat from the barnacles sticking to the hull at least once a week; we looked to do this in the hottest part of the day, so as to cool down a little in the water.

16:00 We try to talk with Jenny almost every day and from time to time with our sisters, brothers, grannies, granddads, uncles, aunts, cousins and other relatives and friends. When storms brew up and we're fighting currents we call Valeri daily. Those minutes on the satellite phone are some of the nicest moments of the day, because they connect us to home and our nearest and dearest.

In the initial days, as we were getting accustomed to managing the boat in the big waves and strong winds we regularly talked to Ralph also.

18:00 We try to send a short email once a day with news about our voyage and a picture, which Jenny uploads on to our blog on Facebook and Instagram. She regularly reminds us that we're not filming and writing enough, and she's certainly right.

20:00 Max has the sunset shift. We have time to enjoy the sunsets in peace. We eat one after the other. We talk about all sorts of topics and joke.

22:00 The last shift of the day falls to me. Full Zen.

This simple regime, cleansed of the stress of the fast paced city life, is actually very healthy for one's psyche, despite the ocean's unfamiliarity, unpredictability and ferocity. When you begin your two-hour rowing shift you know that no urgent email or appointment will interrupt you. After the initial adaptation to this way of life, which took a few weeks, the days began to merge imperceptibly. We didn't even count them – we didn't scratch marks on the wall, as some sailors or prisoners do. In this way we felt freer and more unencumbered by the thought of passing time. When we calculated how many days had passed from the start of our voyage, we always discovered that more days had passed than we expected.

Chapter 22

THE FIRST 1600 NAUTICAL MILES (3000 KILOMETRES) 25 JULY 2020, STEFAN

Whoopee! We passed 1600 nautical miles (3000 kilometres) in 31 days – half of our planned route from Portugal to Brazil. We'd been travelling on average 97 kilometres per 24 hours, or more than 100 kilometres if we subtract the three nights we spent on the drogue, due to bad weather. This distance equalled more than one marathon per rower per day and it took place in the most variable weather conditions, on a boat weighing 1100 kilograms.

In the previous several days, we tried to increase our motivation to row those endless kilometres, imagining that the midpoint was a summit, which we were climbing like mountaineers, before turning and setting off back home. We were telling ourselves that the second half had to be easier, although we knew that in the mountains the way down from the peak was often more treacherous. We promised ourselves therefore, to be at least twice as careful, right up until the end. We also dreamt of seeing much bigger fish than before because we still had to enter ever deeper waters.

Max often said, "Come on, let's talk about something!" Never mind what the time was – day or night – and never mind how tired I was, I couldn't let this chance slip by. He talked to me of his views about the future – how machines with artificial intelligence will penetrate our everyday reality ever deeper, but how there'd be people whose job would be to keep them under close scrutiny, so that the machines or the people who programmed them, would not be able to harm humankind. He asked all kinds of questions – about my work in banks, about what this or that profession involved, about the meaning of hedge fund, investment fund, etc., about events from his childhood, which he didn't remember. For example, I told him how when he was less than one year old and he was learning to walk, we were staying at his Grandma Zoya's and Granddad Serafim's villa in Simeonovo, along with his older cousins, Sophia and Alex Schachne. Sophia was climbing up and down on the three steps between the two parts of the living room and Max was watching her with undisguised interest. He wanted to climb to the upper space, but he was little and the steps were steep. He struggled with them all evening until finally he managed to get up them, he sat on the top step, and proudly clapped his hands, saying in English with a Brazilian accent, "Biggy Max".

Although during the first month of our voyage, we were constantly caught in a survival routine, we began gradually to get used to life on the ocean and feel calmer and more confident – what sailors call 'finding your sea legs'. The fact that we kept most of the letters we had received from friends and relatives unopened, was proof that we had not surrendered to fear or panic and had not reached the limits of our capabilities. Up to this moment we'd only opened a letter from Lara – on her birthday, the 16th of June – so as to feel closer to her on this special day. Her letter really made us melt with tenderness. Even before opening the other letters, they were warming our hearts. The support and love of the people close to you is an extremely strong motivator in such moments. It makes you not only become stronger in the battles with the elements and inner fears, but also feel that whatever happens in professional, sporting and everyday situations, your nearest and dearest will be together with you forever, while these situations will fade and the greater part of them will be completely forgotten or discounted.

During the voyage, we had no access to the internet or social media. Almost every day, through the satellite hotspot, we would send an email to Jenny with one or two photos, which she would upload to our NEVEREST OCEAN ROW profiles on Facebook and Instagram. In this way, friends could follow what was happening with us, and we could reach more people who might decide to become potential organ donors after their death. In the beginning, posts reached dozens but later on, hundreds of people. And then tens of thousands and, towards the end of our voyage, hundreds of thousands of people, mostly from Bulgaria, but also from around the world. Jenny sent us, via email, comments and good wishes from friends and relatives as well as innumerable well-wishers whom we'd never met before. We were amazed and extremely grateful for the waves of words of encouragement which began to pour over us, and charge us with 'nuclear fuel'. This helped us to continue our row tirelessly, day and night and to boldly battle with all the difficulties that obstructed our path. We began to feel that our expedition was not just an adventure or a whim. The support from people we knew and those we had never met, made us believe the expedition was something significant, something for Bulgaria, especially during the unforeseeably difficult time of the coronavirus pandemic. We were representing our country in this first attempt by a Bulgarian rowing boat to cross the ocean, and this gave us wings.

RUBBISH ON BOARD
MAX

It's incredible how much rubbish humans generate. Even in our little boat, we began to be swamped in rubbish. We'd decided not to leave any trace of our expedition in the ocean, so we conscientiously arranged the used lyophilized food packets in one bag and all the other wrappers of bars, cheeses, nuts, dried fruit, etc. – in another. When these bags filled up, we stored them in the spaces under the deck, so we could dispose of them when we got to dry land. Even though we washed almost every packet, there was still some organic material left in them, which began to rot and in the holds, tiny maggots appeared. They didn't bother us because they stayed in the holds with the rubbish, but after the stopover in Lanzarote, little flies had boarded the boat and they began to breed actively and fly everywhere. Luckily, they focused on the rubbish and surprisingly hardly ever landed on us or the fresh food, which we'd opened or were preparing.

Sometimes I decided to decrease their population with my own hands and despite knowing that I wouldn't eliminate them all, I managed to liquidate 20 or 30 flies, maybe more. When I was fast asleep, from time to time a fly would land on my face or body which would immediately wake me up. I felt compelled to find and kill it. It wasn't nice, but I was fed up with being pestered. There were days in which I executed over 100 flies. It seemed to me that if I stopped doing this, the situation in the boat would be intolerable. My father didn't care a jot and he wasn't interested in hunting them one by one, but he did accept some mass killing sprees. Whenever we experienced heavy tropical rain, we opened the big hold on the port side of the boat where we kept the open food provisions, we took out and washed every food packet, poured masses of water into the empty space, bailed out the water with a hand-bailer and returned all the packets to the hold. At these times, the heavy rain would wash the flies into the ocean preventing them from entering the cabin. Of course, there were some living flies left in the other holds and the population continued to exist and multiply. In spite of this, the idea was a step forward towards a calmer future.

DAMAGE TO THE RUDDER
STEFAN

Despite stabilising the electrical system, we decided not to switch on the autopilot because we'd now got used to managing the rudder without it, with the help of ropes – something unthinkable at the beginning of the voyage. One of the two reasons for stopping off in Lanzarote was to fix the autopilot management system, and now we did not even consider switching it on! However, our peace of mind did not continue for long. One day, while we were travelling with moderate winds and waves, a wave bashed the rudder, it juddered and broke.

Our steering system was made up of:

1. A fibreglass rudder blade, sunk into the water;
2. A box made of composite material, similar to plastic, which fastens the rudder blade to the stern of the boat through two metal pintles
3. A metal frame which fastens the plastic box to the autopilot and to ropes for manual control.

We'd made the metal frame ourselves, following our own design and the rudder blade and box we had bought from the innovative Latvian company Dotan, and up to this moment we were really pleased with the products. The upper pintle of the composite box had now broken off and the box itself had cracked. The rudder was an exceptionally important part of the boat, so we'd taken a whole back-up system, including blade, box and metal frame. We quickly installed the reserve system and set about mending the broken one by:

1. Changing the four screws that attached the pintle plate to the box, with four bolts, which should hold the pintle more firmly – screws can be more easily torn out as they only hold the composite by their thread, whereas a bolt has a nut on the other side of the box wall.

2. Installing two metal plates – on each side, between the box and the metal frame, the cracked box between them, so as to reduce the likelihood it would fall apart completely.

Not two days passed however, when exactly the same thing happened with the new rudder box. Once again we fixed the broken box, but this time with four plates of stainless steel, which we took from the scuppers where they held the rubber flaps, which were not of real importance. We fixed the broken pintle back to the box with four four-millimetre bolts, replacing the original screws torn out by the collision with the wave. When the first box broke, we assumed that the composite material had been pretty worn down by the crashing waves in the first month of our voyage. When the second box broke so soon after the first one however, we reconsidered the situation and came to the conclusion that the fault lay with the fact that the rudder had been locked immovably by the control-ropes.

When we used the autopilot, it compensated for the pressure over the rudder by turning it from side to side as the boat was turned by the waves attacking it from port or starboard. It was no accident therefore, that for the first month of the voyage with the autopilot, the rudder had not broken, and when using the rope-controls, the rudder broke in just a few days.

We had no choice but to switch on the autopilot again and continue ahead. We sought to avoid travelling at a big angle to the wind and waves, so as to lessen the chance of the complete disintegration of the rudder boxes, both of which were now cracked and therefore more vulnerable. Of course, this was not always possible, especially in a stormier sea when the waves and wind came from different directions. This would complicate navigation and make our course more zigzag, but we had to take the necessary steps to preserve our rudder through the remaining 1500+ nautical miles (2700 kilometres) to the end of our voyage.

Chapter 23

We continued to enjoy encouraging words from friends and strangers who followed our expedition from dry land via the YB3 tracker, which showed our position every six hours, along with the postings which my mother uploaded on Facebook and Instagram. Sometimes they asked questions which she collected and sent to us. Here are some of them along with our answers:

You talk a lot about the boat, the weather, etc. but what would you say about your health? How do your bodies cope, particularly your hands?

We started as absolute beginner rowers 18 months ago, so we had a lot of catching up to do – by the end of our preparation we accumulated over 7000 kilometres (the planned distance of our Atlantic voyage) of rowing training in gyms and at home. This way, our hands got enough blisters and calluses during training that now on the voyage, this is not a problem. It's interesting that our bodies have switched into survival mode, suppressing pains, wounds and discomfort so as to increase the chance of getting to the opposite shore. For example, when we get back pain or when a knee pops or an elbow swells, these complaints pass within a few hours or days.

The greatest discomfort is caused by our sit-me-down parts. I hadn't planned to mention anything on this topic, but since you asked – let's be upfront – one of us got a small crater in that area, and the other three boils. After applying creams and sprays over a period of days and weeks the wounds healed. Doctor Kalin Dimitrov (the expedition's head doctor, Stefan's brother and my uncle, orthopaedic traumatologist and surgeon) had prepared for us a huge first aid box, which we hope will serve in most situations.

Why did you choose organ donation as your cause?

As you might know, almost every ocean rower has a charitable cause which they support. In the beginning we thought of raising money for different charities, but once we realised the potential of saving lives through organ donation, and that it was simply a case of education and promoting awareness rather than heavy financial donations, we felt this cause was at the heart of who we were. We took on supporting the Ministry of Health's campaign Yes! To life! with no hesitation. The laws in Bulgaria are such that the closest kin to the deceased have the last word, so it really would help if people made an educated decision about what happens to their organs and shared it with their kin. There are the necessary specialists and hospitals in Bulgaria, the basic problem is lack of donors. This is actually the situation globally too. Collectively, we can help with the solution and really save human lives.

What item/device with you on board has been the most necessary and what was irrelevant/unused?

The watermaker (desalinator) is without doubt the most useful item we are carrying. As we need about 12 litres of drinkable water a day, the lack of a machine to purify salt water (electric or manual) would make the ocean crossing almost impossible, because there's no way that we could carry on board a sufficient quantity of potable water for the whole voyage.

On the other hand, the thing we haven't touched since starting out, is our binoculars. The AIS system and chartplotter do a fantastic job in locating the positions of ships around us and notify us of their course and position in real time. Until now everything on the horizon is seen quite well enough without binoculars.

What was the most difficult moment and how did it pan out?

The most difficult moment so far was when the rudder and the spare rudder broke within days of each other when we'd scarcely passed the halfway point of our voyage. We feared that we might be forced to send out an SOS signal or face being carried by the sea winds and currents for months on end. Without a functioning rudder it would have been exceptionally difficult to direct the boat in the continually changing sea conditions over the 1600+ nautical miles ahead of us. Both outcomes seemed extremely unpleasant to us at the time but fortunately, we managed to fix both rudders and we hope they'll last out to the end of our journey.

Stefan, how do you feel about the thought that you're putting your son in danger?

I believe we're not taking a much bigger life threatening risk, than if we'd taken a trip in the mountains or embarked on a journey by car or plane.

I'm reassured by the fact that in the history of ocean rowing, there's been only one event where a boat with two rowers lost its crew and this happened 60 years ago, when the means of navigation and communication were not as advanced as they are today.

Every similar undertaking requires long dedicated preparation and we had thought over, discussed, tested, trained on and corrected dozens of aspects of the ocean crossing in a rowing boat and we felt prepared to take them on. We had also planned several contingency scenarios on how to act in case of different disasters.

What is your philosophy regarding risk management?

This is a many-sided philosophy and practicality which we worked on, throughout the last year and a half:

1. We fed off the experience of the world's most experienced sailors and ocean rowers, with whom we conducted detailed conversations on the subject of identifying and minimising most risks.

2. We endeavoured to make our boat as strong as possible and to get to know its every part –

that's why at the very beginning, we made the decision to build it ourselves and that's why it's a few hundred kilograms heavier than necessary, because of several additional layers of fibreglass, built-in stainless-steel plates, insulation, etc.

3. We've taken spare parts for almost everything on board (for some elements not just one or two but six or more) and we fix everything that breaks as quickly as possible, before the weather gets worse.

4. We strictly follow particular rules like, for example, we are always tied to the boat when there's wind, we keep the hatches closed in bad weather and we avoid unnecessary risks.

5. When weather conditions make rowing too dangerous, we cast the para anchor into the water and wait in the cabin or on deck for the weather to improve.

6. During the voyage, we depend on a fantastic support team on dry land, including Jenny Ivanova, Ralph Tuijn, Valeri Petrov and Doctor Kalin Dimitrov, who all provide us with invaluable support.

INTERVIEWS DURING THE VOYAGE
STEFAN

In the name of the campaign Yes! To life!, we had accepted engagements with journalists from several respected media outlets like Bulgarian National Radio,

BG Radio and Darik Radio, the weekly Kapital and the daily Dnevnik to hold interviews via satellite telephone during the voyage. It was not always easy to maintain a clear connection though. The signal often cut out or muted when the satellites hid behind thick cloud; sometimes the contact made by the cable from the satellite antenna to the telephone began to fail, so that there was no way of talking from the cabin; and when it was raining on deck or strong wind was blowing, we'd barely hear each other. Due to these limitations we agreed for the interviews to be recorded and not broadcast live over the airwaves. Sometimes while we were talking to journalists, some alarm would go off on the boat, a flying fish would land in one of our laps or a tropical downpour would be unleashed. This made the conversations more emotional and funny, at least for us on the boat. Of course, the subject of donorship was more important than anything and we made every effort not to spoil the interviews, so we could reach more people and create a basis for further discussions.

More and more people realised that their decision to become organ donors after their death could give a chance to more than one person to live, to make their dreams come true, to sail. It wasn't just a question of an abstract appeal, 'Be good!', but a concrete cause-and-effect link: if more people took the decision to become potential donors, this would save the lives of more people.

Chapter 24

NEVEREST BREAKFAST
STEFAN

Usually the day would start after the dawn in good spirits, with music blaring loud from the speakers on deck, and with our favourite NEVEREST breakfast:
- 130 g. porridge or muesli;
- 50 g. nuts;
- 50 g. dried fruit;
- 50 g. peanut butter;
- 20 g. vegetable proteins;
- Plus something else as a luxury – cocoa, crema catalana, crushed raw bar – mixed with hot or cold water and well stirred. Sometimes instead of this breakfast we'd eat lyophilized scrambled eggs.

During our shifts between breakfast, lunch and supper, as well as during the night, we'd eat raw bars, sweets, nuts, dried fruit and very occasionally some chocolate dessert. At lunch and supper we'd usually eat lyophilized soup and some basic meal which we'd mix with water, heated up on the gas-ring, and on hotter days with water at the ocean's temperature –

about 26-28 degrees Celsius. When we caught a big fish, which usually happened at night, we filleted it and ate it raw as sashimi for breakfast while it was quite fresh, and for lunch we made fish soup from what was left. Eating two meals of fish was a good use of resources (the fish were over a metre long) and provided us with fresh protein – vital for maintaining our body weight and muscle. It also minimised the use of our lyophilized food which we liked to reserve in case of an extended time on the ocean. On such days we swapped the meal order and for supper we ate our favourite NEVEREST breakfast instead.

I really liked to prepare food for the pair of us, especially our breakfasts. I usually improvised with ingredients and added different surprises to the meals – for example, slices of hard cheese, olives, etc. and I'd add water to the lyophilized portions by eye. I liked Max preparing the lunches and suppers even more, not only because he calculated the optimum amount of water for the lyophilized meals down to the millilitre, but because I melted at the thought that he was taking care of me as well as of himself. I saw how with every passing day of the voyage, with finding the solution to every single problem, and the conquest of every difficulty, Max was growing into a calm, thoughtful and positive human being.

We divided all the tasks on the boat equally, not like father and son, but like partners. Max didn't shy from responsibility, on the contrary – on his own initiative he checked weather forecasts, put forward course changes for discussion, asked our navigators questions, suggested changes in the distribution of the remaining food long before it began to run out, etc.

LAUNDRY
STEFAN

The time comes for any human, however well he lives, to think about laundry. At home the only machine, which I did not understand the workings of and didn't dare come near, was the washing machine. I've always been worried that I'd dye the whole wash with pink, blue or green shades, coming from some rogue item in the machine. As this happened to my wife and my mother, there was no way it wouldn't happen to a laundry amateur like me.

On board NEVEREST we were equipped with a bucket especially for laundry, but we put off its use until it became unavoidable. We purposefully wore as few clothes as possible and we hung them up to 'air' on the lines tied to each side of the deck which we held on to, so as not to fall overboard. In spite of this, Max began to call a pair of blue socks 'blue death', some black boxers 'black death', a grey hat 'grey death', etc. We deliberately did not rinse our clothes in seawater as Ralph had warned us that afterwards it would be extremely difficult to get the sea salt out of them. It was inevitable that our clothes got soaked with sea water however, because waves broke over us while on deck; afterwards they could almost never be completely dried. That's because salt crystals are hygroscopic (tending to absorb moisture from air) and we were just feet away from the water surface.

The washing technique we had thought up was to pour one or two litres of drinking water and a little liquid soap into the bucket, put in two or three items of clothing and squeeze them by hand, so that the water ran through their fabric. After that, we threw away the water and repeated this procedure three to four times. It was incredible what brown-grey liquid came out of not just the first bucket, but from the second and even the third. There wasn't much dust on the ocean except during the time we were rowing close to the African shore, so I guess the grey-brown colour came from the dead skin cells on our bodies mixed with the sun cream, which we covered ourselves in several times a day!

We'd taken with us two liquid soap dispensers – one was quite ordinary, from a 1 lev shop and scented lilac, the other was a special soap, first produced in 1848, by the legendary American company Dr. Bronner's. According to the company's advertisement, this soap was suitable for 18 purposes: for the face, body, hair, bath, shaving, teeth, foot-soaking, inhalation, plates, laundry, floors, windows, general cleaning, makeup removal, rinsing fruit and vegetables, washing household pets, protection for plants from insects and ant dispersal. Unfortunately, with one careless bath the Dr. Bronner's dispenser was washed overboard by a wave and we had to begin using the ordinary soap with the hint of lilac for these multitude of purposes. I can't say whether there was any difference between these two soaps. What was worse was that we had to spend more than a month with only half a dispenser of this liquid soap and so we had to use it sparingly – just a few drops at a time as if they were eye drops.

When we hung out the washing on the lines, the boat looked like the balcony of a panel block in a Sofia neighbourhood during the weekend. When the wind picked up, we had to take down the clothes, so as not to lose them to the sea. When tropical rain fell, we deliberately left them on the lines so they were hit with another rinse, always welcome!

Chapter 25

By now we'd rowed about 2100 nautical miles (4000 kilometres), two thirds of the planned distance to Brazil and I was getting more and more curious about the country where I was born but which I had left too young to have any memories of. My father would play Brazilian music more and more often – rock, bossa nova, samba, axé, etc. and translated the lyrics for me from Portuguese to Bulgarian. Usually the songs were about love and strong emotions.

We were following the situation with the coronavirus in Brazil which was becoming ever more unstable and unpredictable, particularly in the northern region where we had to land and where international flights began to be cancelled. Meanwhile, strong southeastern winds were battering the northern coastline of South America and made our passage to the Brazilian shore almost impossible. For this reason, we decided to change our final destination point from Fortaleza, Brazil to Cayenne, French Guiana. This step would add about 215 nautical miles (400 kilometres) to our route, as well as put us in a more complex situation with strong swirling currents in the region around Cayenne. On the other hand, the prevailing winds were expected to be more favourable in the direction of Cayenne than that of Fortaleza. Even so, we kept a spark of hope that if the situation with winds, currents and coronavirus improved significantly over the next few weeks, we would attempt to land in the northwest end of this exciting and immense country where I was born.

HEADWINDS
9 AUGUST 2020, MAX

Over the last few days the winds around us were weak (below 10 knots – i.e. under 18.5 kilometres per hour) and the waves quite small. That being said, the winds were continually changing direction, often blowing straight at us or from the side of the boat and decreasing our speed to 1 knot (1.8 kilometres per hour) or even less. This was not dangerous, but it hampered our ability to keep to our desired course. Furthermore, it rendered meaningless the energy we threw into the rowing. So we decided to cast the Jordan anchor behind the boat for a few hours and catch up with some sleep in the cabin. It was likely we'd be forced to do this again and again in the days to come.

THE FIRST TROPICAL STORM
13 AUGUST 2020, MAX

We'd read some books on meteorology which explained how tropical storms and hurricanes formed in the Atlantic. Usually they happen close to the Equator, not far from the African coast. When the damp air, heated up by the warm water of the ocean, begins to quickly rise upwards, it creates low atmospheric pressure and the air from the surrounding high pressure areas begins to move towards the low pressure area, to warm up and also be lifted up higher. The moisture in the rising air condenses with the lowering temperature and creates clouds and rain downpours. Because the Earth is revolving around its axis, a vortex is created in a circle around the rising airmass – anti-clockwise in the northern hemisphere, clockwise in the southern one. The vortex created in this way, also called an anticyclone, gathers even greater speed especially round its higher edges as it reaches the higher strata of the atmosphere. In the centre of the anticyclone, also called 'the eye', the wind speed is low but out on its margins, the speed can reach dangerous levels. If the speed of the wind exceeds 64 knots (119 kilometres per hour), the storm is classified as a hurricane in the Atlantic Ocean; as a typhoon in the North Pacific; and as a cyclone in the South Pacific and Indian Oceans. The diameter of an anticyclone can reach hundreds of nautical miles, and the anticyclone itself can travel thousands of nautical miles.

Our navigators followed the development of tropical storms and hurricanes around us and warned us if any of them were getting close. On the 11th of August the first tropical storm, Josephine, headed for us. We didn't come up with that name. The World Meteorological organisation decides on the names of tropical storms and hurricanes in the Atlantic from a previously prepared lists of male and female names which get changed every six years.

When Josephine began to approach us, rowing became impossible and we had to cast the para anchor. In the beginning the wind pushed us north, after that back to the east, and then to the south. We had to shelter in the cabin and to keep the hatch closed to stop water getting in. On account of the cabin's thick insulation, when the two of us were inside it only took minutes for the temperature to rise relentlessly because of the heat given off our bodies, and for us to start sweating profusely, as if in a sauna. Puddles formed beneath us. It became stifling. We had to open the hatch from time to time for a few seconds so a little fresh air could come in, but we couldn't keep it wide open. We were constantly waking up from the lack of fresh air, the heat and the rocking of the boat. I had hoped that when the storm came, we could at least rest from the rowing and sleep, but as it happened, our sleep was reduced to even shorter intervals than on a normal day's rowing with changeovers every two hours. On top of everything else, the wind pushed us back 20 nautical miles (about 37 kilometres). We carried on with the para anchor for almost two days – most of the time shut up in the cabin while the boat, tossed and engulfed by the waves, bucked non-stop like a horse that had just had reins put on him for the first time. We realised we were far away from any kind of other seagoing vessel, not just because we didn't see them on the horizon or the chartplotter, but because big boats are provided with detailed weather forecasts spanning days and weeks ahead and can travel at a speed of 15 to 20 knots or more. They are able to easily change course and avoid the bad storms, which meant that the stronger the storm, the more unlikely that any big ship would pass close to us. It might sound paradoxical, but our rowing boat had to manage with worse conditions than bigger vessels. Thus, during the storm I had many thoughts going around in my head – fear for our lives and the state of the boat, the thrill generated by the elements, pride that we were hanging on in a situation similar to those in films; where the end of the world seems to be imminent and, last but not least, relief that at last we might catch up a little with sleep and rest.

The day the storm passed, my father got down to fishing and this time caught a neon-blue mahi-mahi, almost a metre long and weighing about three kilograms. By now he'd begun to manage the intricacies of filleting and made sashimi from the mahi-mahi that very few restaurants in the world could compete with – so fresh that it was almost still moving, cut into generous thick slices and divinely flavoured with a few drops of soy sauce.

WEATHER FORECAST
STEFAN

Every day we downloaded on our mobile phones weather forecasts from PredictWind through our Iridium GO! satellite hotspot. They included animated models and data about the wind, the waves, etc. from several sources. These forecasts were very useful in our course planning and corrections, which we discussed with Valeri and Ralph. Of course, they often differed from the actual atmospheric and sea conditions, as sometimes the wind blew from the opposite direction to that expected. The forecast got updated several times a day and covered the following 14 days. In practice however, we could only depend on them for two or three days ahead.

If we wanted to travel south, and in the next days a north-easterly wind was expected, followed by a north-westerly, instead of fighting the wind too much, to keep course exactly to the south, we could afford to deviate slightly to the west, expecting after that to be brought back east by the gusts.

If the speed of the wind was over 10 knots, it pushed us in the direction it was blowing and we could diverge no more than 30 or 45 degrees at the most, to the right or left. This meant that if the wind was blowing from the north, we could only travel south, a little to the southeast or southwest, but not directly east or west, and certainly not north. This also meant that if something or someone fell off the boat, even in moderate wind, the rower could not return to fetch it or him. With a man overboard, the best strategy was for the rower to immediately throw out a rescue rope or a drogue, and hope that his fellow is a good swimmer. If one of us were to fall overboard, and not be noticed immediately, his only hope would be to press the red button of his PLB (Personal Locator Beacon) tied to his belt, which would send an emergency signal through the satellites and wait for some ship, located close by, to be dispatched by the closest rescue centre.

HEADWINDS
17 AUGUST 2020, MAX

For two whole days, we rowed into headwinds of about 10 knots. It was like pushing a car that doesn't want to start. We could not last long this way and we had to stop from time to time, to gather our strength. When the work of rowing against the wind became unbearably heavy, we cast the para anchor and collapsed on the mats to sleep for a few hours. When you are on dry land, if you stop to rest, you carry on from the spot that you stopped. In the sea however, if you stop rowing, the wind and the current immediately start pushing you backwards or sideways from the course, even if you've cast the drogue. That's why we always aimed at reducing our stops on the drogue to a minimum – we set the alarm clock for one to two hours and got up to check whether the wind had died down or changed its direction.

Chapter 26

PROBLEMS WITH THE RUDDER ONCE AGAIN
18 AUGUST 2020, STEFAN

On account of the strong headwinds, we'd cast the drogue from NEVEREST's prow, which kept the boat turned against the wind and waves, as was expected. As usual, it was tossed left and right and up and down by the waves and at some point we heard a loud noise from the stern. The rudder was again broken. Despite the two pairs of four-millimetre bolts with which we had screwed down the plate of the upper pintle, fastening the rudder to the stern of the boat, the composite material of the plate had been shattered and the rudder was thrashing furiously, hanging only off the lower pintle which held it to the stern.

I shouted to Max to get me the pliers and I threw myself into saving the rudder before its lower pintle twisted off the ring attached to the stern on which it was held, or before the second pintle got broken. We managed to take it off in time with only a broken upper pintle. Both stern rings were undamaged. It was just as well we'd made each of the rings from two three-millimetre plates of stainless steel which we'd fixed with bolts through the stern of the boat before covering them with more layers of fibreglass.

We took out the spare parts bag in which there were all kinds of supporting elements, bolts, brackets, cables and goodness knows what else – just in case we needed to carry out repairs on the boat during the voyage. We also had a comprehensive toolkit on board comprising things like pliers, spanners, screwdrivers, hacksaw, hand drill, etc. We tried to fit all kinds of combinations of brackets, plates and bolts to once again fasten the broken pintle to the rudder box. One of the stainless metal brackets fitted like a glove over the pintle's cylindrical shape. We just had to cut a five or six-centimetre slot into the rudder box through which to push a plate, which we'd taken from one of the stern U-bolts and to tighten the bracket to the plate with bolts. The result was perfect – the repaired rudder looked like a broken human limb, which was supported by bolts and plates to hold it still, until it mended. It seemed to me that after this repair the rudder was stronger than it had been at the beginning of the voyage.

The repair took a few days, meanwhile we rowed with the spare rudder. Although we tried to protect it as much as possible – we avoided rowing at a wide angle to the waves and tried to prevent the boat from rotating which would put strain on the rudder, after a day or two the spare rudder happened to break the upper pintle a second time. This was the fourth rudder breakdown since the beginning of the voyage, in spite of all our efforts to protect it. We now took off the rudder with every casting of the drogue to avoid its being continuously bashed into the rubber stops fixed to the stern.

The moment came to test the strength of the rudder repaired with the bracket, plate and bolts. After we installed it, I got down to making a similar repair to the spare rudder, so it would be handy if we needed it. We were now experts at fixing rudders and believed that there'd always be a way to keep the rudders in working order until the end of the voyage!

The fifth rudder breakdown was surprising – the six-millimetre bolt screwed into the metal frame of the rudder, to which we connected the autopilot, snapped in two. Clearly the strains on the construction of the rudder were significant. Fortunately, this damage was the easiest to fix. It took us literally one or two minutes to unscrew the nut and replace the broken bolt with a new one.

Apparently, the use of a box made of a composite material similar to plastic, for the support of the rudder blade on an ocean rowing boat, was really not a good idea. This might do the job on small sailing boats – of the 'Optimist' class, for which Dotan rudders were intended, but clearly not for ocean rowing boats weighing more than a ton, bashed and turned about by huge waves. Instead of using the original box of composite material, before the launch we should have fixed up the rudder blade and autopilot with the help of a sturdy metal frame only.

When I think about how many dozens of times we took out and put back the tools, spare parts and fastening elements, I feel sick. We kept them in the hold behind the cabin, right on top of all the luggage, so they'd be close at hand. As they didn't fit into one bag, we'd divided them into two, and goodness knows by what law in nature, but when we looked for one specific tool, fuse or bolt, it was almost inevitably not in the first bag we checked but always in the second. The tools themselves and spare parts which were not made of stainless steel for sea conditions (AISI 316), gradually began to rust. The pliers barely opened and closed. Just as well we took the universal lubricating spray, WD 40, with the help of which we managed to revive and unscrew rusted bolts. If you manage to find rust resistant tools and spare parts, don't hesitate to take them to sea instead of their ordinary metal equivalents.

PERPETUUM MOBILE
STEFAN

Sometimes our rowing seemed infinitely long. An average sport training session lasts less than an hour. Imagine that after a two-hour session, you can rest for two hours and after that have to do another two-hour session – this would probably seem too much. If later there follows a third two-hour session, this would be overdoing it, wouldn't it? Then if you had to do six sessions a day, it might seem to you like sadism. And now imagine a whole week under this regime. How about a whole month? And three months? It seems impossible. Actually it isn't. Humans are infinitely adaptable animals and almost infinitely endurable. There are other mammals who are a lot stronger or a lot faster than humans. There is no other mammal however, able to endure more than a human. Since prehistoric times humans have followed, hunted and exhausted animals to death.

During our preparation we only did up to three training sessions on the rowing machine a day at home, and our training sessions on NEVEREST lasted 24 or 48 hours at most. At the time, we felt that they exhausted us almost to the limit. In fact it could not have been even close to the limit because when we were on the ocean, our routine included 12 hours of rowing a day each, our bodies entered a state of per-petuum mobile. Providing we continued to eat and rest regularly between the two-hour shifts, we felt we could go on forever this way.

Somehow the body adapts itself to increase its chance of survival. From time to time, our waists or our knees hurt or some boil or sore formed, but in-stead of the pain stopping us completely, it passed in minutes or hours. The brain still sent out pain signals to make us aware we should take it easy and protect the hurt part of the body, but it didn't debilitate us for whole days or weeks – it clearly knew that we couldn't afford it.

Instead of being in constant agony, we fell into a Zen state in which we felt a spiritual tranquillity, a quiet joy and an inner strength. Of course, unpredict-able, stressful, dangerous and funny situations were continually cropping up, which temporarily took us out of this state, but once we had coped with them, the sense of satisfaction returned us back to our in-ner comfort. Once we'd got used to night rowing we spent fabulous nights under the stars and moonlight, sunk deep in thoughts about life, the immediate and distant future. I remember how one night I put on Beethoven's 'Moonlight Sonata', while Max rowed un-der the huge moon and clean sky through calm wa-ters – an unforgettable moment of quiet joy. These unique and magical moments are better shared with a loved one – then the joy is doubled.

We learned to listen to the signals our bodies sent us and to try to distinguish the causes of indisposition. For example, one of my hamstring muscles (the muscle in the back of the thigh) began hurting from time to time. It was not engaged in the active and arduous phase of rowing, in the straightening of the legs, when the blades of the oars caught the water. It was used in the folding of the legs at the knees, as you pull the sliding seat towards your ankles. I discovered that this muscle hurt me when the weight in the boat wasn't distributed properly and the prow was pointing downwards. In principle the deck ought to be slanted at 1or 2 degrees towards the stern, and not towards the prow. Then the boat has less resistance to the water, the sliding seat moves downwards, and not upwards, when it returns to the ankles and the hamstring muscles are less stressed.

FURTHEST DISTANCE AWAY FROM THE NEAREST COAST
16 AUGUST 2020, MAX

Days, weeks and months before the start of our expedition across the Atlantic Ocean, there was something related to our voyage which really bothered me. I asked myself how I'd manage with total isolation and distance from civilization, from familiar things and people. I wondered how this isolation might turn out to be a problem that would be hard to overcome, and so I wanted to be prepared for my encounter with this feeling during the voyage. From seafarers' tales, I knew that with the lengthening of time spent at sea and the monotony of everyday life, the days begin to look longer and time itself seems to pass more slowly. The thought that dry land is so far away and unreachable, and life on the land is happening, as if in another dimension, was surely going to torment me. I knew that the moment would come when we would be so far away from dry land, that the astronauts in the International Space Station would actually be our closest neighbours.

Well, I did experience this feeling but fortunately it wasn't a problem. We'd been at sea for 53 days and the surrounding ocean, with its infinite horizon, noisy restlessness, and unfathomable depths, was like a familiar presence, alive and comforting. It made no difference whether we were 100 or 1500 nautical miles from the nearest land. The fears had disappeared. I had adapted.

Chapter 27

Our experienced navigators – ocean rowers and sea-dogs told us that in the last weeks the Intertropical Convergence Zone had moved about 10 degrees – i.e. about 600 nautical miles to the north, bringing with it powerful south-easterly trade winds. Ralph and Valeri had discussed the subject at great length, and Ralph had talked with another two experienced ocean rowers, who had been his navigators several times during his voyages. They were convinced that for this reason, as well as the powerful Gulf Stream which was more than 100 nautical miles (185 kilometres) wide and travelled from east to west along the northern coast of South America, it would be impossible for an ocean rowing boat to reach Cayenne in the next few weeks. Only Valeri mentioned that there was a remote chance of its success, but only if the winds died down and we had tremendous luck navigating between the vortices of the ocean's currents.

For this reason we had to give French Guiana a miss and continue moving west. We decided not to

land in the neighbouring countries, Surinam or Guyana in light of the various uncertainties associated
with them. Due to the coronavirus pandemic, their
marinas and airports were closed and it wasn't clear
when we'd be able to return to Bulgaria, even if we
managed to reach them. So our new plan was to land
in Venezuela – as the official final point of our transoceanic voyage, in order that it be recognised by The
Ocean Rowing Society as the first two person rowing
boat crossing from the European to the South American continent. We'd read however, that in Venezuela
at that moment, complete chaos reigned: dictator-
ship, famine, petrol shortages, crime, etc. That's why
we decided we would not stay in Venezuela after all,
but would immediately row to its neighbouring country, Trinidad and Tobago, where we could meet Jenny,
Lara and eventually others who might come to greet
us. After that, we would ship NEVEREST in a container back to Bulgaria and catch a flight home.

This would add over 1000 kilometres to our already planned 6000 kilometres course from Portugal
to Brazil, more than 7000 kilometres in all.

We decided to gather our strength, to redistribute
our food and to do more fishing. This meant more
pleasures, more unknowns and a greater sense of
achievement when we finally finished our adventure.
Spirits on board NEVEREST continued to be high!

— 246 —

ROWING SOUTH
17 AUGUST 2020, MAX

The wind stabilised for a few days, then regrettably instead of blowing from the east to help us travel west towards Venezuela, it came from the opposite direction – mostly from the west-northwest. For the greater part of the year, the trade winds blow from the east, especially during the winter when the South Atlantic is at its calmest but at that moment they were not!

Instead of rowing directly against the wind or casting anchor and drifting back towards the east-southeast, we decided to go south. We reckoned that if we managed to slip sufficiently to the south – for example, to 2 or 3 degrees north latitude, we might still have a chance of reaching French Guiana. Hopes in vain – only after a few days we found ourselves in the midst of a new tropical storm, Laura, which again whipped winds up from different directions and forced us to cast the drogue and sit it out.

We'd already got through one tropical storm and the forecast for this one was no scarier than for the previous one, so we weren't frightened for the boat or ourselves this time. We knew however, that several tense days moored to the drogue awaited us along with the inevitable drag-back. A week later, after Laura had passed and entered the Bay of Mexico, it gathered additional strength and turned into a Category 4 hurricane with a maximum wind speed of

159 mph (240 kilometres per hour). Subsequently, it entered Louisiana as the strongest hurricane passing through the state since 1856. We were lucky it didn't develop earlier.

RAIN
STEFAN

People normally hide from rain – under eaves, umbrellas, raincoats. Being drenched by rain is usually annoying and unpleasant. In the first days of the voyage when the rains were cold and continuous, we also protected ourselves in waterproof jackets and trousers and sheltered in the cabin, hoping we wouldn't get wet. We'd heard of tropical rain which would saturate us every day and honestly we didn't look forward to them.

When we reached the tropics however, it turned out that clouds and rain were our saviours from the sun's burning rays and the roasting air's embrace. I began to summon them and look forward to them. When some rain cloud appeared on the horizon, I hoped it would make for us and according to who-knows-what law of physics NEVEREST attracted them, so that almost every rain cloud passed exactly over us. I reminded Max to wake me if rain was approaching the boat when I was asleep, so that I could immediately get out on deck to cool down and wash in the crystal clean rain drops. When it was raining in a strong wind or storm, the rain drops flew almost horizontally and stabbed our skin and eyes like needles. It was painful and sometimes impossible to open one's eyes in the direction from which the wind and rain were coming. At that moment I put on goggles and tightened them with a strap behind my head, so they didn't fly off into the sea. I'd taken goggles with completely transparent plastic lenses, meant for a motorcycle, which were most suitable for this, since they did not darken further, the already dark atmosphere during the rain, and since there was no way they could break into dangerous glass fragments.

We encountered basically two types of rain – 'shower stalls' and 'celestial coverings'. We called shower stalls, the separate rain clouds which floated in an otherwise blue sky and from which streams of water poured, similar to a shower. Sometimes they passed over us in a matter of minutes and sometimes lasted an hour or two. Celestial coverings then, were huge fronts with grey clouds that covered the whole sky and from which rain poured for days on end. Sometimes because of these downpours, the solar panels were unable to charge the batteries sufficiently, and for a couple of days we had to postpone the use of some electrical devices on board like the stereo, the radio station, the watermaker, etc.

As the temperature of the air under the thick rain clouds was lower than that surrounding them, when such a cloud came towards us, the wind always strengthened by 5 to 15 knots, sometimes more and often changed its course. In the beginning we thought that it happened out of nowhere, but we quickly got used to this phenomenon and expected it. It was even fun – it was as if you're entering a mini storm with the boat that could last a few minutes or a few hours. We tried to see off these mini storms without casting the drogue and most of the time we managed to hold the line.

At the end of one of the radio interviews from the boat with BG Radio, my favourite presenter Simo (Simeon Kolev) heartily wished us a cloudless sky to the end of our voyage. He clearly had no idea how pleasant and helpful ocean clouds could be, because without them the heat of the burning sun would be intolerable!

MY 48TH BIRTHDAY
24 AUGUST 2020, STEFAN

We originally thought that by the time our birthdays came – mine on the 24th and Max's on the 25th of August – we'd have finished the expedition and so we hadn't prepared special treats, candles or presents for each other. In spite of this, I'll surely remember my 48th birthday until the end of my life, unlike many others, which merge together in my memory.

Immediately after midnight passed and my rowing shift finished, I got down to fishing. The school of fish which day and night swam alongside NEVEREST, now numbered dozens of fish and it literally took me two minutes to catch the biggest mahi-mahi we'd seen until now. It was certainly longer than a metre and weighed at least four kilograms. It was a divinely beautiful specimen with silvery-bluish nuances. The sashimi from it was as thick as a finger and as tender as lamb's brain.

In the morning there came a complete calm and the surface of the sea turned into a mirror, reflecting the oars, the clouds and the sun. I had dreamt of coming across such a windless calm and I melted from the peace and beauty around. With the lifting of the oars from the water, small circles of miniature ripples formed – like steps in the snow, which along with the traces from the rudder left a trail behind the boat for as far as the eye could see.

Contrary to any other time, Max and I put on trunks and jumped into the water together, so we could take pictures with the video camera of each of us swimming amongst schools of blue, green, black, grey and brown fish. Max made somersaults under the water and moved smoothly like an astronaut in low gravity. Then he darted around with quick strokes here left, there right, up and down like a bird dancing in the skies. For me it was most enjoyable to join the school of mahi-mahi and to swim round the boat, as if I was also a fish in the sea.

In the afternoon in this utterly windless place, we felt the greatest heat since the beginning of the voyage – almost 40 degrees Celsius in the shade. As if by order a shower stall turned up and drenched us with miraculous rain. The rain soon passed and the sun burned down some more, but after a short while, the wind turned 180 degrees and the same shower stall returned and washed us one more time.

It was a truly wonderful and treasured birthday and I was happy that the celebration would not end on this day because as always, we would be continuing the festivities for Max's birthday.

MY 17TH BIRTHDAY
25TH AUGUST 2020, MAX

I got to turn 17, but I did not feel like a birthday boy. Maybe because I wasn't surrounded by friends or because when you do the same thing every day, it's as if time has stopped and you find yourself in a parallel reality. That's why I decided to break our daily routine and reward myself on this day. Usually, we ate whatever was in the packets we grabbed on the day. This time though I took five food packets and selected the tastiest meals for lunch and supper. After ten minutes of deliberating, I decided that the menu would consist of chicken tikka masala for lunch and farfalle with spinach for supper.

It turns out that food can be a huge motivator in any arduous undertaking. We'd been on the water for over two months and it wasn't that I'd lost hope, but it was still hard to swallow the fact that there was a lot of distance left to the finish. For this reason, every day I enjoyed the arrival of lunch or supper, because I felt rewarded for the whole day and night's rowing. The fact that I valued and looked forward to small things gave me a psychological boost and the strength to continue to row and row, far from my friends and family on dry land.

I wasn't angry or disappointed that I could not celebrate my birthday in the normal way. Yes, I wanted to see my friends, I wanted to celebrate with my sister and mother, I wanted to get presents and to have some fun, but the fact was that this was impossible and I accepted the reality of the situation and didn't complain or get annoyed. You could say that I looked at the situation positively, after all not many people could say that they'd celebrated their birthday in an ocean rowing boat in the middle of the Atlantic Ocean. I felt lucky.

My mother sent me hundreds of good wishes and words of support from relatives, friends and strangers who were following our expedition which had been posted via the social media platforms. All these messages lifted our morale and encouraged us in this difficult period. We'd never received so much positive energy from so many well-wishers. This showed me that when someone decides to follow a great dream, they can receive much more support than they expected.

THE INTERTROPICAL CONVERGENCE ZONE
AUGUST - SEPTEMBER 2020, STEFAN

The Intertropical Convergence Zone is the region of dead calm between the north and south trade winds, where the wind ought not to be horizontal, but vertical. It is not fixed and it expands and contracts and travels north, south, east and west. This zone, also called the Doldrums, was infamous for the fact that many sailing boats and ships have loitered in it for weeks, their food provisions dwindling away. Our impression of our stay within it, was that there was seldom any dead calm for more than a few hours and for the most part weak winds of 5 to 10 knots blew from constantly changing directions.

Little waves arose which travelled chaotically. This caused us quite some difficulty, in that the boat would rock in all directions disrupting the rhythm of rowing. The wind pushed NEVEREST hither and thither, sometimes strongly enough to divert us from our chosen course or even keep us in one place, no matter how hard we rowed. For this reason we were often forced to cast the drogue and wait for the conditions to improve – sometimes several times a day.

It wasn't dangerous but it was exhausting. Of course, we looked to use these unplanned stops to swim with the exotic fish, to catch up with sleep, to talk with our nearest and dearest on the phone, to enjoy each other's company, to eat together face to face instead of one after the other, which was usually the case when one is rowing and the other is resting. If only it had been cooler!

THE INESCAPABLE HEAT
MAX

During the voyage some people asked us about the temperatures around us. My two Grannies – Karina and Zoya, were especially concerned – they worried that we'd either be too cold or too hot. Their biggest worry was that we'd get sunstroke. On the 14th of June, on our launch from Portimão, Portugal the temperature of the water was 18 degrees and the air temperature was 28 degrees Celsius in the shade. On the 20th of August when we again measured the temperature at 9° N (9 degrees north latitude) – several hundred nautical miles north of South America the temperature of the water was 28 degrees and of the air – 34 degrees Celsius.

On sunny days the air temperature on board in the shade reached 38 to 40 degrees, but it felt like 45 degrees or more – especially when there was no wind. When you row in such temperatures, sweat pours from your body and from time to time everything around you starts to spin before your eyes. In order to protect ourselves from serious sunburn, we regularly applied sun cream, alas this contributed to the unpleasant feeling of stickiness. Usually I rowed in boxer shorts only, and while I was resting I got as naked as when my mother bore me. My father insisted we wear sun-resistant T-shirts and apply sun cream to our arms and legs at least twice a day, so we didn't burn up or provoke more serious problems like skin cancer. When it was his turn to rest, he also undressed and quickly snuck into the cabin for a deserved relaxation. Thus at least in those moments, our bodies and especially our bottoms had a chance to dry out from the damp which had become our constant travel companion.

According to the rules of The Ocean Rowing Society, stretching a canopy over the rower was not allowed, because it could serve as a sail, which would help move the boat faster. Actually not just one or two ocean rowing boats were detected and filmed with unfurled sails between upright oars. We, however, had taken the firm decision not to engage in such unsportsmanlike tricks and in no way to compromise our voyage with breaking any rules.

Sometimes as I was rowing under the sun's merciless burning rays, I dreamt of the moment when my shift would finish and I could shelter in the shade of the cabin to rest, rocked by the waves. In reality, I'd collapse into the hot cabin, where the temperature would be higher than on deck, due to the lack of draught, the thick insulation and the greenhouse effect, created by the hatch. I felt as if I was being roasted over a grill while on deck and that I'd entered a hot sauna when in the cabin. It was good that we had taken screens of aluminium foil, which are normally used on a car windshield to reduce the greenhouse effect. We cut them into the shapes of all the hatches and fastened them with double-sided scotch tape or elastic bands to protect ourselves at least a little from the suffocating heat.

The closer we got to the Equator, the hotter it became, we took every opportunity to jump into the water for one or two minutes to cool down before entering the cabin.

THE STRUGGLE WITH CURRENTS
28 AUGUST - 4 SEPTEMBER 2020, STEFAN

While we were rowing west, we discovered that we were struggling with a current which was moving to the southeast at 0.7-1.3 knots (1.3-2.3 kilometres per hour) and was hampering our progress in the desired direction. When there was no current or wind, we could row at a speed of 2-2.5 knots (3.6-4.6 kilometres per hour). In recent days, however, we advanced at hardly 0.1-1.5 knots (0.2-2.7 kilometres per hour).

When we stopped rowing even for a little – for example, to drink some water, we immediately began drifting southeast. The same happened when we cast the drogue – the current pushed it together with the boat to the southeast. For this reason we continued rowing, even when we were scarcely moving in the right direction.

The mapping and forecasts of oceanic currents are a lot more imprecise than those of winds, as they are based on mathematical models, created on the basis of satellite findings on pressure and temperature, and not on the actual movement of water mass. As can be seen from the two maps of currents in the region in which we were rowing, at the same moment the representations of the currents in the two maps, created by Nullschool and Windy show almost nothing in common. As though they'd been made about two completely different regions (see figure 4 in the Photo Insert).

On Valeri's suggestion, we began to stop rowing for a minute every four hours in order to measure the speed and direction of the wind and the direction of the boat's drift, with the oars dipped motionless in the water; so as to establish which of the current models was closer to reality. It turned out that the first map from Nullschool was more accurate. What was interesting, was that the Gulf Stream current seemed to have made a complete U-turn and instead of helping us, was hampering our movement westward. Clearly in the hurricane season, not only the winds but the currents went crazy too.

In the beginning, Valeri told us that in order to go around the current that was pushing us south-east, we had to make for the north until we reached 10° N. This meant us rowing 78 nautical miles (144 kilometres) north without getting any closer to our final destination, and only then turning west towards it. When we got to 10° N and were about to celebrate however, it turned out that we hadn't got around the current and we had to row north at least another 30 nautical miles (55 kilometres) to 10°30' N. It seemed to us that this rowing against the current and with changing winds and chaotic waves had no end. When we reached 10°24' N, a new tropical storm broke out which made rowing impossible and once again we had to dance in a circle on the drogue.

We were so close to the elusive 10°30' N, where we hoped to see the back of the current – at less than 6 nautical miles (11 kilometres), but the storm pushed us back south by about 13 nautical miles (24 kilometres), which we had gained through a lot of sweat and pain. We were in a trap:

- It wasn't a good idea to row west, because the deeper we entered the current, which moved southeast, the more it strengthened. Even if we'd managed to cross it, a few hundred kilometres to the west we'd have fallen into an even stronger current originating from the Gulf Stream, which also travelled southeast but at 3-4 knots, and we couldn't pass through it by rowing.

- It wasn't wise to row too much to the north, because the further north we went the deeper we entered the hurricane region and the greater the chance of a hurricane running into us and tearing the boat to pieces.

- If we went south, we'd hit the southern trade winds, which would send us back to the north-west.
- There was no point in rowing east because we'd be moving in precisely the opposite direction to that of our destination point and there'd be the danger of the winds carrying us back to Africa.

When I took part in marathons and ultramarathons in town or in the mountains, I always had a fixed and foreseeable end goal. Even when I joined the Bulgarian Lions team in the 300-kilometre UTMB-PTL course in the Alps, however difficult the terrain and considerable lack of sleep, I could still say to myself – there's only 82 kilometres or just about 20 hours left – or something similar. In this trap on the ocean in which we found ourselves however, there was no light at the end of the tunnel. There was no way of being sure what the final destination point of our voyage would be. Even if we were to agree that this would be the island of Trinidad, we couldn't know how many circuits were left to do through storms and currents before getting there. Our trajectory through the ocean in the last weeks looked more like the flight of a butterfly than the purposeful course from point A to point B. There was no way to extrapolate an average speed over the remaining distance and take that as a marker of how much more we had to row to the finish. Quite hypothetically – if all winds stopped blowing and all currents disappeared, it would take us about half a month to reach Trinidad. If we took into account what distance we'd travelled westwards in the last half a month and continued to travel in the same direction at the same tempo, we'd need more than two months to get there and we had food on board for a month at most.

THUNDERSTORMS
28 SEPTEMBER 2020, STEFAN

During the night there were lightning flashes in the distance. In the beginning they were far away and without thunder, but it wasn't long before we started hearing the rumble of accompanying thunder. As a child, I'd heard that if you count the seconds between the lightning flash and its thunder, you could tell roughly how many kilometres away from you the lightning strikes the ground. We weren't sure whether this method was accurate, but we could use it to learn if the thunderstorm was moving towards or away from us.

And so between the first lightning flash and its thunder we counted 66 seconds, with the second 33 seconds, the third 16, then 8, then 4. At this moment we stopped rowing and feverishly began to put together a lightning conductor from materials at hand. Amongst the spare parts which we'd brought on board we found a four-square millimetre insulated cable – two short pieces of about a metre and a half each. Separately they were too short, so we joined them together and wrapped the connection with insulation tape. We stripped each end of the cable – we planned to fasten one end to the spare metal antenna and for this we made a loop from the bare wires and the other end we dipped in the ocean – where the electrical charge would disperse.

By this time the lightning began to flash not only on the starboard side of the boat as in the beginning, but from all sides – we were clearly in the middle of the storm. We'd heard that lightning could bore big holes in yachts' fibreglass hulls while at sea. Also we'd heard that sometimes lightning, which had struck water metres away from yachts, gave off such strong electrical charges that they burnt out some of the on-board navigation and communication devices. Of course, we'd also heard about incidents when lightning hit people on the ground – some of whom died on the spot, and others survived by a miracle. We feared that there was a big chance that a lightning strike would hit the boat, not least because it was the only object on the water, in an area of hundreds of nautical miles but also because there were metal objects on it like antennas, pipes, plates, etc.

As we got the lightning conductor cable ready to attach to the spare antenna, we heard it emit a hissing noise and saw that on its tip, a purple sphere had formed, on the surface of which mini-lightning bolts flashed. Because we hadn't noticed our boat being hit by the lightning, we thought this was caused by the electrical charge in the air around us, created by the thunderstorm. The spare antenna was not connected to the boat's electrical system, so the charge could go nowhere but this effect lasted a long time after the passing of the storm. We couldn't work out how strong the charge in the antenna was. We worried that it might have reached hundreds of volts and that if we touched the antenna with the cable we could get an electric shock. So we waited until morning and after the effect had passed, we installed the lightning conductor by hand. When our friends on land heard about the phenomenon of this crowning charge on our antenna, they told us that other seafarers had described a similar effect which they called St. Elmo's fire – after St. Elmo, protector of sailors according to Catholic belief. It's considered by sailors to be a good omen.

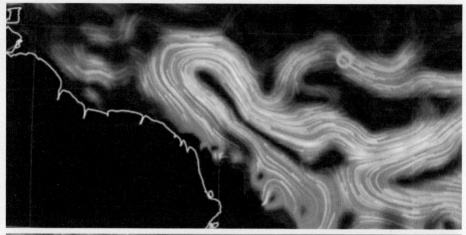
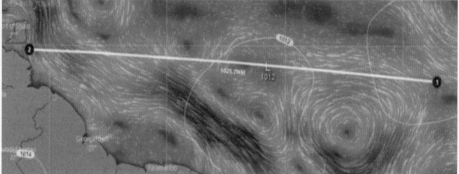

Fig. 4 Map of the currents – the colours indicate the speed of water movement from blue (slowest) through green, orange, red to purple (fastest)

Yes! To life! is at the heart of our expedition

Joy at reaching dry land after months in the ocean (Barbados)

When you discover your favourite food (Chicken Tikka Masala) amongst the packets of lyophilized meals

Mahi-mahi – a present from the ocean for my birthday

Trying to catch fish with a knife

Gourmet sashimi

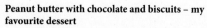

Fish + bouillon + gas stove = fish soup

Peanut butter with chocolate and biscuits – my favourite dessert

Max pretending to be serious

Latest rudder repairs

The traffic around Gibraltar keeps us alert

Casting the Jordan series drogue

Retrieving the para anchor after a storm

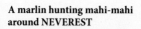

A marlin hunting mahi-mahi around NEVEREST

Cleaning the boat of barnacles

Diving with wild ocean fish

Countless mahi-mahi

A moment of freedom and relaxation

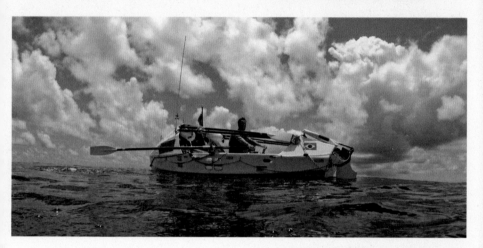

A rare moment of calm ocean waters

Chocho and Tina's last moments together

Another tropical storm in the Atlantic

	SWELL 2
	1.4m. 9s.
WIND 26kt.	1.9m. 9s. SWELL

| TUE | WED | THU | FRI | SAT | SU |

| TUESDAY 15 | WED |

🕐	0	3	6	9	12	15	18	21	0
kt	⇗ 20	⇗ 27	⇗ 23	⇗ 26	⇗ 26	⇗ 25	⇗ 24	⇗ 21	⇗ 20
	27	30	37	35	37	35	36	32	31

In the tail of Hurricane Teddy

The joy of rowing in the ocean

Wave-hills

In nature's embrace during a tropical storm

Amidst Hurricane Teddy

105 different sunsets

Soaked but happy

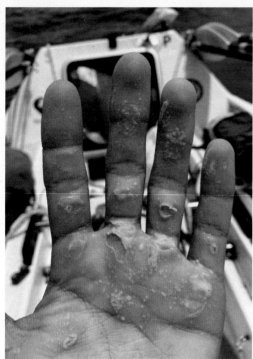

Sometimes in the storms you 'send back' your supper

Countless blisters

Three hours a day on the manual watermaker becomes a bit too much

Max before and after the voyage: minus 14 kg

Stefan before and after the voyage: minus 10 kg

Jenny and Lara meet us in Barbados

Portugal – Barbados 4444 nautical miles in 105 days

A moment after arriving in Barbados

Certificates from Guinness World Records

Happy together

Chapter 28

A PSYCHOLOGICAL COPING STRATEGY
MAX

Even before the launch, I'd prepared myself psychologically for the difficult moments, critical situations and enormous obstacles which we'd encounter. I didn't believe though, that there would be a danger of finding ourselves in such a trap that our journey's final exit would be so unclear. I think I'm a positive realist i.e. I like to be as positive as I can be within the margins of reality. My father on the other hand is a complete optimist, this for me is one of the reasons that we made such a good team on the boat. Apart from the positive attitude on board, there was something else which allowed me to live through this stage of the crossing, without despairing or thinking I was going mad.

As usual I was listening to a podcast, while I rowed through the night. This one was about American prisoners of war in Vietnam. When they were imprisoned, most of the soldiers thought that they'd be rescued in a matter of months, by Easter. Easter came and went. Then they hoped that they'd be rescued by Christmas. Christmas came and went. The same thing happened with the following Easter and Christmas, and so on over a period of five years. This sounded really nightmarish and I asked myself what a person goes through faced with such a situation, what coping mechanism could be worked out. The podcast guest explained that most of the soldiers didn't manage to survive those five years of imprisonment because of their delusional hopes. Every holiday was met with indescribable disappointment, which crushed them even more. One of them decided to take a different approach. He refused to count the passing weeks and months rejecting this crushing optimism. Most of all he stopped marking the time and associating rescue with a specific date or period. What he did not reject was the idea that someday he would be rescued and once again be free.

I told myself that this mechanism could be applied to my situation and that the message related to me perfectly. I did exactly that, I isolated myself from all external factors and gained a constant neutral state. This allowed me to not despair or get stressed, no matter what situation befell me. I knew that someday we would reach dry land, irrespective of how many storms, breakdowns or course changes awaited us. I knew that all that was expected of me was simply to row and survive. I felt how this new attitude brought about real changes in my behaviour. For example, when my father announced the latest unpleasant news that headwinds would continue for three or even seven more days, this didn't affect me in any way. I simply replied, "Fine, whatever, it doesn't matter". I told myself that in headwinds and following winds I'd still be rowing and life would still carry on, no matter what was happening around me. That's how I was able to isolate myself from the nasty feeling which came from a seemingly insurmountable obstacle.

OUR SATELLITE HOTSPOT STOPS WORKING
5 SEPTEMBER 2020, MAX

One jolly day our satellite hotspot device, Iridium GO! suddenly fell out of kilter. Every day we downloaded weather forecasts through it, sent and received emails and pictures and if our satellite phone was faulty, we were able to use it for chats through the satellites via our mobile phones. The device began to restart only after a couple of minutes and fell into a non-stop initialising cycle, so in practice we couldn't use it for sending and receiving data, nor for voice functions. We talked over the satellite phone with teams from Range Global, PredictWind and Iridium and we made goodness knows how many attempts to resurrect the device to life, through restarting, taking out the batteries and sim cards, drying in the sun (although the device had never left the cabin and had not been splashed with water). Maybe the moisture in the air or something else had influenced this malfunction, but no matter what we tried, we didn't manage to fix it.

Unfortunately for us and to the disappointment of our friends who were following the blog and our social media pages, we couldn't send photographs through our normal satellite phone. Also we couldn't download animated weather forecasts on our phones. Just as well, Valeri took to sending us short emails to our YB3 tracker with wind and wave forecasts.

Up to this moment, we'd travelled 3250 nautical miles (6020 kilometres) in 74 days on the ocean. This was more than the distance we'd originally planned to travel from Portugal to Brazil! What remained was at least another 1100 nautical miles (2000 kilometres). Again we were moored to the drogue because of winds of 10 to 20+ knots coming from the west and southwest, caused by a third tropical storm, Paulette, since the start of the voyage.

We expected to spend at least another one to two days at anchor before renewing our rowing. It was like déjà vu – in the previous month we'd already been in this situation twice. Paulette passed us and a few weeks later on the 13th of September, it gathered strength and turned into a hurricane. Lucky for us, by that time it was far away. It's no surprise that not one rowing boat has crossed the Atlantic Ocean from Europe to South America, entirely during the hurricane season. This time we'd tied both drogues to NEVEREST's prow in order to decrease the drift back eastward to a minimum, but despite this, the boat was slowly carried east and it was jumping in the waves like a wild horse which refuses to be tamed. Around this time, it happened that both my father and I fell asleep while rowing and bashed our heads into the spare oars, tied to both sides of the boat. Not surprising as we were only getting a maximum of five hours sleep every 24 hours. That's why during our stops on the drogue, we tried to catch up with sleep as best we could. This time the wind took us back 36 nautical miles (67 kilometres) and forced us to grab the oars, even before the storm had passed completely. It took us three days of tireless rowing and struggle against the current, winds and waves to cover this distance again.

THE DOLPHINS
STEFAN

Often while we were rowing, dolphins appeared and accompanied us for hours on end day or night. It was beautiful and exciting to watch two or three and sometimes more than a dozen dolphins emerge and dive, rhythmically in perfect sync and to hear them exhale over the water like humans. Sometimes they jumped so high that their entire bodies left the water. Once while I was rowing especially energetically and the boat was moving faster than usual, I saw the dolphins who were following us in the distance. Each had something pink around its mouth, but I could not distinguish what it was. I joked with Max that the dolphins were left panting with their tongues out by the chase after the boat, although it was exactly the opposite – they'd surely got bored by our slow pace.

A little later, when we'd cast the drogue I could not resist the temptation, and despite the wind and surrounding waves I jumped in to swim with the dolphins. I aimed a small video camera at them. Sadly however, instead of coming to swim together, they dived and disappeared into the deep dark blue ocean. Probably the smell of an ocean rower was not to their taste.

HURRICANE TEDDY
15 SEPTEMBER 2020, MAX

It was the 15th of September and my fellow pupils would be starting the new school year. The summer holiday always seemed too short to me and I never wanted it to end and the new school year to start. From the time we rowed out from Portugal on the 14th of June, three months had passed and to be honest, by now I was yearning for my friends and the atmosphere at school. For the first time I wanted my summer holiday to be over and to start going to school every day.

On the 15th of September in the Atlantic Ocean however, we found ourselves in the midst of the latest tropical storm which the National Hurricane Centre in Miami forecast would develop into a hurricane on the 16th of September i.e. the maximum wind speed within it was expected to exceed 74 mph (64 knots or 119 kilometres per hour). The name of this hurricane was Teddy. By a quirk of fate, from the time my father was born, close relatives and friends called him Teddy even though his name was Stefan. Clearly the name wasn't close to my Grannie Karina's heart – it came from her father-in-law – so she had thought up this nickname. And to this day I don't know if this was the name of some friend or a character from a favourite book or film of hers. She'd say that she doesn't remember, which sounds suspicious to me.

Valeri had warned us several days in advance of storm Teddy's approach and the likelihood it would turn into a hurricane. The French Guiana coast guard also got in contact with us via my mother, whose telephone number was registered with our boat's identification MMSI number, so they could ask us if we'd like them to organise a rescue operation. We were situated too far from the shore for them to send a rescue boat from there, but they could signal some merchant ship located closer to us, and send it to take us on board. Of course, with such a rescue, we would have to leave NEVEREST to its fate in the ocean and hope that someday we could collect it from whatever shore it lands on.

The coast guard warned us that we'd have to make a decision within 24 hours – a few days before the hurricane fell on us because during a big storm rescues in the ocean were very difficult or just plain impossible. Even big ships were forced to keep a course at a narrow angle to the wind and waves and might not be in a position to move towards a vessel in distress. Moreover, even if they managed to get to us, it would be extremely difficult for us to climb on board during a big storm, which would either crash the boat into the ship or distance it.

From the moment we'd begun planning our North Atlantic Ocean expedition, we'd prepared ourselves psychologically for the fact that we'd collide with big storms. Up until now, we'd got through three storms without emergencies and incidents and we had no intention of raising a white flag. My father and I reasoned that however terrifying and uncomfortable the prospect of the hurricane passing through us, it could damage the boat, but there was no way it could sink it. Apart from that, a rowing boat like NEVEREST has a lot fewer things that can break in a hurricane compared to a yacht with a mast, sails, rigging, centreboard and whatever else. At the end of the day, if we couldn't continue our voyage with NEVEREST after the hurricane we'd look for help then and not beforehand. We were feeling a healthy dose of curiosity about what would happen during the passage of the hurricane. Surely it would be an unforgettable experience.

This did not mean however, that we sat with our arms crossed to wait for the hurricane to be upon us. In conversations with Valeri, we sharpened up our strategy – we had to move as quickly as possible from the place we were at – 11°30' N and 45°16' W, in a south-westerly direction in order to distance ourselves from the probable trajectory of the hurricane. At the same time we ought not to go further south than 10°30' N, because we'd probably get too deep into the south-easterly current with which we had battled for weeks on end beforehand. Meanwhile we took out the 50-litre waterproof emergency bag from the big hold in which from the very beginning we'd put important things like a medicine bag, watermaker, compass, signal rockets, knife, etc. and we added water, food, documents, passports etc. The idea was that if we were forced to evacuate NEVEREST in our inflatable life-raft, it had to be easy for us to grab the most essential stuff. Apart from that we divided the dozens of items which we'd stuffed into the nets on the cabin walls into three piles:
- items which we would leave in the nets – like toothbrushes, toothpaste, torch, compass for determining wind direction, etc.

Maxim and Stefan Ivanov

- items which we hadn't used from the beginning of the voyage and which we put in a bag marked 'deep freeze'
- items which we might need in the next few days, but which would better be removed from the nets, so we didn't hurt ourselves on their edges in the expected rocking of the boat – like pegs, camera tripods, sun glasses, etc. or which shouldn't get wet, in case the boat capsized and water got into the cabin – like documents, spare phones, etc. We put these items in a waterproof bag for 'temporary freezing'

It was very exciting to row, running away from the hurricane – facing the stern, expecting every moment black clouds to emerge on the horizon along with storm bearing winds which could turn the world inside out. After 26 hours, the wind began to gradually strengthen and rowing became impossible. We'd reached 10°50' N – i.e. we'd moved 40 nautical miles (72 kilometres) to the south. We cast the drogue and as we expected the south-easterly current took us and we carried on moving to the southeast, until we reached 10°45' N. After that the wind direction turned from southwest and we gradually began to return back to the northeast.

The winds around us continued to strengthen and the waves became ever more tumultuous and bigger. Most of the time we were bolted inside our cabin capsule and it felt like giants were kicking and playing football with it while we were trying to sleep, drowning in puddles of sweat. A result of lying on sweat-soaked mats was that we began to feel little nips on our skins – it was as if we'd been breeding fleas on board which were now biting our backs and not giving us a moment's peace. After we washed the mats a few times with drinking water and wet wipes and bathed in rain, the 'fleas' disappeared. I suppose they hadn't existed – simply our skin had erupted from the long baths in our own sweat.

From time to time, we got out of the cabin to cool down and admire the spectacle of the elements that raged around us. The wind was whistling and lifting spray from the waves around. Rain was falling horizontally, the drops stabbed our bodies like darts making them tingle. Occasionally the boat's prow was submerged under a wave and this washed over the cabin. Another time the waves came at our side and swept over the boat sidewise. In comparison with the cold wet wind, the waves were pleasantly warm. We just had to hold tight to the ropes, so they didn't knock us over on the deck or sweep us overboard. Adrenaline was screaming in our ears and racing through our bodies; we were in the grip of a horror train and felt the might of nature with all our senses. We were happy that NEVEREST was coping with the situation without a problem and it was as if it was actually enjoying itself, like us. The only thing that wasn't clear was how much more the hurricane would grow in strength and what could change in the situation around us. After it passed us, hurricane Teddy reached Category 4 with winds of up to 140 mph (220 kilometres per hour)!

Mum had looked through the online database of the Ocean Rowing Society from the first rowing boat voyage in 1896 to the present day and she had found out that if we managed to complete our voyage, NEVEREST would be the FIRST rowing boat, crossing the

Atlantic Ocean from east to west entirely in the hurricane season, which officially begins on the 1st of June and finishes on the 30th of November.

I asked myself whether I'd have preferred to row without storms and hurricanes over the exhilaration we were experiencing at the moment. However difficult and frightening it was, I have to admit that I wouldn't exchange this voyage through storms, hurricanes, currents and dead calms, for a voyage in ideal conditions in a different season, even if we could have set a record for the quickest rowing boat crossing of the Atlantic Ocean.

Chapter 29

Hurricane Teddy gradually moved off to the north-west. We'd survived! NEVEREST was unbreakable – what a joy!

Once again, we grabbed the oars and for the first eight hours while we were being bashed by bigger waves, we rowed with no rudder, because apparently it was pretty fragile. After that, we installed it but we'd clearly been in too much of a hurry, because the waves' commotion had not calmed down sufficiently and it broke for the sixth time. The breakage was exactly as the fifth one – the six-millimetre bolt, screwed into the metal rudder frame to which we'd strung the autopilot arm, snapped in two. It took us a minute or two to unscrew the nut from the broken bolt and change it for a new one. Although we tried to protect these rudders like newly laid eggs, they continued to break. There was no question that once we landed we would have to change the construction of the fastening of the rudder blade to the boat's stern and to the autopilot, with an entirely metal frame and a thick connecting bolt. It wouldn't be difficult but it had to be done before NEVEREST was ready for new voyages.

BARBADOS — ISLAND OF FIG TREES
21 SEPTEMBER 2020, MAX

We'd travelled 3700 nautical miles (6850 kilometres) and just 800 nautical miles (1500 kilometres) remained to Trinidad and Tobago.

Surinam, Guyana, Venezuela and Trinidad and Tobago continued to be in a COVID isolation regime and their airports were closed to regular flights. Even if my mother had managed to arrange permission for us to land in Venezuela and we'd agreed to travel by land to Caracas or by sea to Trinidad and Tobago, there was no knowing when flights from there to Europe would be renewed. I could not afford an indeterminate period of absence from school, because the 11th Grade awaited me along with really important exams, related to my future.

This made us change the final destination point of our voyage once again and we chose to land in Barbados or Grenada. When we arrived in one of the two island states, we planned to catch the first possible flight to Europe.

Barbados was closer and so we decided to head for it. Because it was north of 13°04' N, however, the island was in the path of hurricanes and tropical storms and so these regularly passed by or through it. I knew that Barbados was situated in the western part of the North Atlantic Ocean, east of the Windward Islands in the Caribbean Sea. And what awaited us on our way there, we would soon find out.

THE AUTOPILOT STOPS WORKING
SEPTEMBER 2020, STEFAN

The autopilot at long last gave up the ghost – its compass stopped working and it froze. One of our greatest fears from the beginning of the voyage was for something like this to happen at night time in the stormiest waves. When the autopilot dies, the rudder gets stuck in a stationary position which could cause the boat to go in a circular trajectory, at some point becoming perpendicular to the waves. In this position there is a high risk of the boat capsizing. Fortunately this didn't happen at night.

We'd brought a spare autopilot because many ocean rowers had complained that their autopilots broke down during their voyages and so in just a few minutes we changed it over. We didn't even have to cast the drogue. In principle, these autopilots are meant for sailing yachts, which move faster and keep a straighter course with their sails, and because of that the autopilot has to make corrections less often. Our poor autopilot had worked for almost three months, only resting from time to time, when we managed the boat with ropes or we were on the drogue. On the advice of ocean rowers, we'd set it up in a regime so it made corrections more slowly and at big course diversions. This clearly helped somewhat, because it still lasted a significant time and didn't overheat as had happened to other rowers. It would be wonderful if one of the autopilot manufacturers made a model meant especially for ocean rowing boats!

SAILFISH AND MARLIN
SEPTEMBER 2020, MAX

One of the fastest fish in the ocean caught up with us – an enormous sailfish, about three metres long. In the beginning we thought we were dealing with a shark, but on examining the video we took underwater, we saw the sailfish in all its size and beauty – including its huge dorsal fin which looked like a sail, unfurled from head to tail. Usually this fin is retracted, but when the fish hunts and attacks its prey, it stands up to stop the smaller fish escaping past it. We wouldn't have wanted to have physical contact with this sea giant. These fish can reach a speed of 59 knots (110 kilometres per hour). The flat long bill in the shape of a sword is no more than a modification of the upper jaw, shaped from the nasal bones. This bill reaches up to one third of the whole body, i.e. about a metre or more.

On one of the hotter days my father, as usual, decided to bathe in the ocean. Because we were now closer to dry land, the chance of encountering a shark had increased. I advised him not to take a dip for the few days necessary to successfully complete our trip, so as not to take unnecessary risks. However, he really insisted on cooling down, because he thought he was on the edge of sunstroke and he agreed a compromise to bathe just for 30 seconds. I continued to be sceptical and told him to be quick in that case. He'd soaped himself from head to toe and for the first time he jumped into the water without putting on diving goggles. I scanned the water and just a few metres from the other side of the boat I saw the body of a shark, at least three or four metres long. I turned to Dad and spoke to him in a really serious voice, "There's a huge shark on the other side of the boat, please get out of the water immediately!" I repeated this twice because he didn't seem to believe me, asking if I was joking. I continued to insist in a serious voice, until he decided to get out ten seconds later. When he stood up on deck and looked around, he saw the huge fish and couldn't believe his eyes. He probably told himself to be on his guard if I warned him of something. He managed to capture the fish on video – it turned out to be a marlin, which looked a lot like a sailfish, but it had a small sharp-tipped fin behind its head instead of a huge sail-like dorsal fin. Seen from above as it passed by the boat, the marlin looked as broad and mighty as a horse – it could easily have skewered my father.

We've seen pictures of two ocean rowing boats, pierced by sailfish or marlin bills. In both cases, their bills had pierced more than a foot into the boat and broken off in spite of being a few inches in width. I imagine how this sword could stab between my ribs as I was sleeping in the cabin.

Chapter 30

FOOD DELIVERY
SEPTEMBER 2020, STEFAN

Our food supplies were beginning to run out in spite of the ocean's generosity in providing us 12 large fish. By the 25th of September we had spent 94 days on the water, while we'd planned for our expedition to take 60 to 90 days at most. We had unopened packets of daily rations for another six days and additional raw bars, sweets, oat desserts, protein bars, gels, dried fruit, nuts and other similar remains from the previous days' packets, which had enough total calories for at least another ten days.

As our progress during the last month had been completely unpredictable, Jenny had got busy searching for a boat from French Guiana to come and tow us ashore or at least bring us some food. In spite of getting in touch with several ports and owners of yacht charter companies, no one showed any readiness to provide such a service. Yachts were packed away and marinas were closed because of the hurricane season and the global coronavirus pandemic.

I thought we didn't need rescuing and that little by little we'd get free of the currents, the dead calm and the troubled winds. After we got out of the Intertropical Convergence Zone, we expected the prevailing winds to come from the east and finally, instead of hampering us they would begin to help us advance west. Although four storms and hurricanes had now pushed us backwards and we had had to row hundreds of nautical miles to get around the currents, after every pushback, we managed to catch up the lost distance and conquer new territory to the west. For weeks on end, we'd begun to save on the lyophilized food by catching fish, dividing into two portions the large size meals and eating lyophilized scrambled eggs for lunch or supper. We could further reduce our calorie intake and catch more fish, so that we wouldn't die of hunger over a longer period. It's a shame we hadn't brought a harpoon – big mistake. If we had, our food provision would have been in the bag, throughout the whole expedition. It was hard to tell how many kilograms we'd shed up to this moment – eight to ten maybe, but we continued to feel good and our strength hadn't started to dissipate.

Of course, one of the most difficult things is to convince your mother that you're not hungry. There was no way Jenny believed that we were not starving. It was a saving grace that at least we succeeded in discouraging her from sending an aircraft carrier or some submarine to take us off the boat. We managed to agree on her only sending us food and a new Iridium GO! satellite hotspot and that would be it. I held out on not involving the rescue services, coast guards and ships in a rescue mission, because our situation was really not calamitous. If Jenny managed to find a sailing boat to bring us additional provisions, Max would be pleased, and she'd be happy to have taken care of us.

That's how our fate crossed paths with David Matelicani, who lived out in the deepest wilds of French Guiana, close to the Surinam border and had a few small sailing boats with which he organised tourist excursions along the South American coast. At the outset, David had no intention of sailing himself and had looked for another seafarer in French Guiana to bring us our parcel. He didn't find anybody who wanted to do it however, so David agreed to sail out to us, but no further than 300 to 400 nautical miles and no further north than the 11th or the 12th parallel where the danger of being caught in storms and hurricanes became greater. Jenny and Max discussed what favourite lyophilized meals from Expedition Foods to send via David, along with whatever else he could buy from the local supermarket – apples, oranges, peanut butter, chocolate paste, biscuits and bread. I remained silent giving them free rein to choose the food, although I felt the quantities were way too big – what they were ordering would last us at least a month and a half!

There were quite a few problems with the dispatch of the food and satellite equipment to the back-of-beyond spot in French Guiana where David lived. Meanwhile a fifth tropical storm, Wilfred, passed over us and in its wake we continued our westward progress. Valeri had told us that once we crossed the 47th meridian, headwinds had to decrease. And it really turned out that way – with every succeeding meridian, which we crossed, our struggle with them diminished. We'd climbed north to about the 12th parallel and the strong currents were to the south of us, although currents still appeared and disappeared, of about 0.5 to 1 knot, in different directions.

David at long last prepared his yacht, Eileen from Avoca, received the food parcel from Expedition Foods and the satellite equipment on loan from Range Global and made the final purchases. His wife was from Trinidad and Tobago and six months earlier had gone there to see her relatives while she was six months pregnant. Meanwhile the country went into lockdown because of COVID-19 and she hadn't been able to return to French Guiana, and so had given birth in Trinidad and Tobago. The baby was now three months old and it still wasn't clear when there'd be renewed flights to this island nation, so that mother and baby could return to dad. An even greater tragedy had befallen David days before his setting out – his mother had died from coronavirus in Italy, but he'd been informed of this only two days after her burial. I don't know whether it was these blows in his life or his seafarer's brave heart that made him take on this voyage. Since he had no one to leave the care of his cat and dog to when he sailed, he took them with him on the yacht and weighed anchor to meet us in the Atlantic!

When we first arranged our meeting in the ocean, we agreed to do it around the 54th meridian somewhere between the 11th and 12th parallels – something like agreeing a date between Mayfair and Park Lane. So as not to miss one another, David activated the reserve satellite hotspot, which he was bringing us, so that we could talk every day on the phone. In addition, a colleague of his from French Guiana sent him our exact coordinates which he received from our tracker four times a day to an additional satellite device. About 640 nautical miles (almost 1200 kilometres) were left to Barbados, and to our meeting place about 320 nautical miles (almost 600 kilometres). David for his part had to sail 400 nautical miles (730 kilometres). He expected that with the current winds and currents in the French Guiana region, which in his view he knew better than any other seafarer, he'd be travelling about 100 nautical miles (185 kilometres) a day.

Everything in the ocean is unpredictable and we reached and passed the 54th meridian. In order not to make David chase us too far, after we passed the 55th meridian we cast the drogue and the combination of currents and winds took us straight northwards. We began to drift almost directly north – from 12°23' N to 12°37' N. David was getting closer to us but his arrival was still delayed because his autopilot had broken down in the bad weather during the night as he was fighting with unfavourable winds. We agreed to weigh anchor and row southwest and after 20 hours, we finally met.

When we made the appointment with David a few days before, Max and I began to discuss how far away we'd be from Barbados when we met David:

- Our optimistic forecast was that we'd meet him earlier – at about 350 nautical miles (650 kilometres) from Barbados, so as to use the additional food and satellite hotspot for more time.

- Our realistic forecast was that we'd meet him at 250 nautical miles (460 kilometres) from Barbados.
- Our pessimistic forecast was that we'd meet him at 180 nautical miles (333 kilometres) from Barbados.

With less than a day left before our meeting, we thought of asking Fiann Paul – the Icelandic ocean rower who held the most records for fastest ocean crossings and for first ocean crossings on some routes and who was also the official coordinator for the Ocean Rowing Society, whether Max's record as the youngest ocean rower would be counted if we received a parcel of food and a satellite device. We sent him an email, which we dictated over the phone to Jenny, saying we needed a definitive answer and if the record wouldn't be counted, we'd turn David around without taking anything whatsoever from him. Fiann answered immediately that receiving this package would not hinder the recognition of the record related to the age of the rower. It would hinder a speed record because in comparing the speeds of different boats, they had to be carrying all their own provisions, but we were not aiming for such a record so there was no problem.

When we met David, we had exactly 250 nautical miles (460 kilometres) to go in a straight line to Barbados.

THE MEETING WITH DAVID
1 OCTOBER 2020, MAX

When we spotted David and his sailing vessel, Eileen from Avoca, we realised that this was the first person and the first yacht we'd seen since leaving Lanzarote 88 days earlier. Clearly most yachtsmen had decided to keep well away from this part of the Atlantic in the hurricane season or had been hampered by the restrictions imposed due to the global coronavirus pandemic. We are truly grateful to David for his bravery in setting sail and his skill in managing the crazy currents and winds around French Guiana at that time of the year.

When he reached us, David lowered his sails and skilfully got within less than ten metres to us, so we could agree to how we'd transfer the provisions from his boat to ours in the choppy sea. He'd brought a plastic kayak for this purpose and suggested he'd load the provisions in it, then pass by us and throw us a rope to which the kayak would be attached. Once we'd caught the one end of the rope, he'd let go of the other end, so that the whole time, the kayak would be held by the rope. And that's what we did.

David distanced himself, loaded the kayak with a huge pile of lyophilized foods and other provisions and passed graciously by us, throwing us the rope. The pile was so big that we assumed that this was the whole parcel. It turned out we had to repeat the operation another four times, until we'd transferred everything my mother had sent. David had decided on his own initiative to add some packs of Red Bull, beers and cakes. A few days before our meeting, my father had lost his stainless steel spoon in the ocean. Just as well that David had two spoons and with no hesitation he threw our way one of them tied with a string to a float, before turning past us one last time and setting off for French Guiana. Otherwise my father would have had to carry on eating with only a fork – he'd had an eruption of herpes on his mouth and I didn't want him to give it to me, if he used my spoon. We managed to spot David's dog which jumped up beside him and looked with some curiosity at us and everything happening around it. Clearly the cat showed no interest in the shouting and what was happening on board, because it did not appear on deck.

THE BIRDS ON THE OCEAN
STEFAN

In some films about shipwrecks, the survivors in the lifeboat somewhere on the ocean, begin to jump for joy when a bird appears over the boat, taking it as a sign that they're getting close to dry land. In reality this may not quite be the case and birds can actually be hundreds, even thousands of miles from land. Throughout our voyage we met up with birds the whole time, even when we were in the middle of the Atlantic Ocean.

One day, after more than two months on the ocean, a bird landed for the first time on the boat.

We named it Eduardo because it probably came from Brazil, which was about 800 nautical miles (1500 kilometres) to the south of us. Eduardo was an inquisitive and fearless swallow. It looked over every part of the boat, including the cabin. It climbed over our arms and heads. It stayed to rest with us for a few hours, gave us some lucky droppings and flew off.

A few days later two more swallows landed on the boat. We called them Tina and Chocho. It was obvious they were crazily in love, as they stayed close to each other and exchanged kisses through their beaks for most of the time.

It seemed they were extremely tired, their eyes were often closing and they didn't touch the water and crumbs which we offered them. In contrast to Eduardo, they stayed on the boat overnight – huddled together a few centimetres from the moving rowing seat. It didn't bother them that our hands holding the oars were swinging over their heads or that the boat was continually being bashed by the waves. In the morning we found Tina laid out on the side, stiff and motionless – she'd died from exhaustion. We laid her in the water and while she was still floating on the surface, some fish grabbed her and she disappeared into the depths. Chocho remained alone, perched on the cabin. He fussed around for about an hour, after which he flew off, dived headfirst into the water and also disappeared.

MONSTROUS FEARS
MAX

Before the day when the idea of this rowing boat expedition occurred to me, I'd never sailed or rowed, I'd never built something as big as an ocean rowing boat and I'd never challenged myself to something as unimaginable as an ocean crossing.

The first monster which I faced was THE FEAR OF THE UNKNOWN. Absolutely everything connected with the challenge of crossing the ocean in a rowing boat was unknown to me. I tried to imagine how we'd be able to manage with just two oars and it was completely inconceivable to me; all the elements and challenges that had to be sorted and overcome, were entirely unbeknown to me; I had no knowledge of how we'd be able to build an ocean rowing boat on our own; I wasn't prepared to communicate with gigantic ships we'd pass in the ocean; I had no experience in traversing ocean waves and winds and currents; I didn't have the nerve to face the media which would likely be interested in the expedition; and I was scared. Of course I was scared. It turned out I had a secret weapon which helped propel me past all the hardship that I faced in the period of voyage preparation – which had lasted for about a year and a half.

I wondered to myself – what motivated me to spend hundreds of hours in rowing training and thousands of hours in the garage building the boat instead of being with my mates. It turns out this was curiosity. It was curiosity that was the voice in the back of my head which whispered to me: "Max, how can you build a boat? Max, how will you feel in the middle of the ocean? Will your rowing skill be up on par, only after a year and a half of preparation?" I wanted answers. That's when I realised I'd created a monster killer, a slayer of fear and this was curiosity. Curiosity led me to the day of departure. Curiosity killed THE FEAR OF THE UNKNOWN.

The second monster which I faced was horrifying. It was THE FEAR FOR MY LIFE. When I was finally on the ocean, there was no way I could feel safe. The boat was constantly rocking due to the bombardment of waves. I had to force myself to eat, to survive, even though I didn't want to put any food in my mouth because I was suffering from seasickness. I had to row 12 hours a day – month after month after month. I had to navigate the boat amongst nine metre high waves. I had to stay locked up in a cage – our cabin was smaller than two square metres, as tropical storms and hurricanes were passing through. All this, and more, made me fear for my life.

The fact that I was exposed to these horrid conditions for such a long time, forced my body to adapt. My mind also adjusted. I developed a sixth sense which told me that it was always time to act and never time to panic. Thus, gradually I began to free myself from the fear for my life. In dangerous situations, instead of giving way to panic, I began to take the conscious decision to work through emerging problems as quickly as possible. That is what made me the master of my destiny and my life. From then on, when I found myself in seemingly dangerous situations, I felt safe. The new knowledge and experience which I'd gained, built on every day, gave me the spear with which I killed the second monster. Experience killed THE FEAR FOR MY LIFE.

The third monster which I met was THE FEAR OF FAILURE. Every ocean rower and every sailor knows that no matter how much you prepare, no matter how many precautions you take, things will start breaking down on the ocean. Our boat began to fill up with hundreds of litres of water every day, forcing us to continually pump it out. Our autopilot, which helped us control the boat, broke down. Our solar panels which generated electrical energy for our communication and navigational devices, corroded. Our rudder which was essential for the boat's navigation broke six times. Every day we had to cope with new problems. We knew that each one of them could have ended our voyage, preventing us from reaching our goals; that it was crucial therefore, again and again to pull up our sleeves and give everything we had to solving every problem. We had to constantly think up more and more new ideas, to set aside time and test each one of them, and to hope that the best one would work. And that's what we did. We didn't allow ourselves to give up or lose heart, we knew that the perseverance and will to find the best solution to every problem would lead us to a successful conclusion.

What motivated me through these difficult moments? Actually it was something which my friend and fellow pupil Ryan Welsh had said to me the day before the voyage: "Max, this is going to be hard. This voyage will be the hardest thing you've done in your life, but don't look at it as an obstacle or a challenge. I think it would be better to take it as a blessing, because you're really lucky to be able to take on and do something like this."

I contemplated these words for days and weeks while we were rowing in the ocean, and I realised that I was grateful for three things: firstly, that so many things had fallen into place to bring about the actualisation of this voyage. If we hadn't succeeded in coping with just one of the many problems we faced, if something hadn't worked as it should have, we wouldn't have been able to set out. Secondly, I was grateful that I had the means and opportunity to take on such a task. I knew that many people could not say the same, and that's why I never allowed myself to take what was happening for granted, I took it as a gift and a lesson. And last but not least, I was grateful that even in the most difficult and darkest moments of the voyage, I wasn't in such a harsh situation as hundreds of other people were at the very same moment. All this made me think: "Stop feeling sorry for yourself. Be grateful for what you're going through, for the fact you're alive and healthy, and have the opportunity to carry out an important mission, a voyage of discovery".

Experiencing this new feeling, the feeling of gratitude to fate, I was no longer a slave to a monstrous fear. I had quenched my thirst for success. Gratitude killed THE FEAR OF FAILURE.

No one is fearless. It's down to each person to determine their approach.

Chapter 31

AND IT SMELLS OF DRY LAND
6 OCTOBER 2020, MAX

There were less than 100 nautical miles (185 kilometres) to Barbados. We'd now got ourselves north, to the 13th parallel, on which the southern shore of the island was located and we carefully checked the weather forecast several times a day. We were worried that we'd miss it if winds and/or currents pushed us too far to the south or north of the island, in that it was quite small – less than 40 kilometres wide. If some tropical storm or hurricane appeared at the last moment, it could wreck us on its coast, what an end to our voyage! Considering that the winds and currents didn't allow our approach to the huge country of Brazil or its neighbour French Guiana, reaching the tiny island of Barbados in the middle of nowhere was by no means an easy task.

My mother and Lara had to take a flight to Barbados. If they arrived too early, Lara would miss more days of school and it still wasn't clear if we'd manage to even get to the island – by now we had already changed our final destination so many times for this or that reason. On the other hand, if they arrived too late, they'd miss our landing on the island and their journey there would have been pointless.

Barbados wanted all arrivals to have done a PCR test for COVID-19 before flying to the island, and to do a second test four days after the first, after their arrival. Between the two tests they had to quarantine in a hotel, without being allowed to leave it. Because both my mother's and sister's tests were negative, they got bracelets which certified that they could leave the hotel.

Land ho!!! On the horizon we saw the contours of land, for the first time in more than three months on the ocean. We felt like real seafaring explorers, who yelled with all their might at the sight of dry land after months of solitary voyaging in the ocean. Excitement and strong emotions flooded our little rowing boat... Barbados, here we come!!! So as to avoid mooring up on the island at night, through the final kilometres we significantly reduced our rowing, and we arranged a meeting with my mother and Lara by the South Point Lighthouse (the lighthouse marking the southernmost tip of Barbados). They had to rent a motorboat, with which they could meet us and if needed tow us to the island, if the wind, currents and waves didn't allow us to reach shore under our own steam.

According to the rules of the Ocean Rowing Society, the crossing of the ocean would still be recorded, if due to bad conditions and dangers, the towing of the boat was not more than 20 nautical miles (36 kilometres) from the mooring point. So one way or the other, we had to get ourselves to within 20 nautical miles of Barbados. We remembered with anxiety the 'Battle for Lanzarote', when we had to row the whole night sideways to the wind and waves and barely managed to get to the island. That's why for some days now we were aiming at Barbados and constantly correcting our course in view of the wind forecasts. We were travelling a little faster than predicted and so as not to have to cast the drogue and wait for the meeting, we spent a very leisurely night before reaching the island. We rowed less, cleaned the boat and made a substantial supper; to celebrate the approaching finale to our voyage, we actually sat opposite one another. This happened very rarely because in our daily routine, one of us ate while the other rowed, with his back to the cabin.

At dawn we were quite close to the island and were travelling along its southern side a few miles from its shore when we began to encounter fishing boats which went out to fish early in the morning. The island fishermen spotted our ocean boat, rowing from the east and waved to us in greeting as well as enthusiastically setting off all the sound signals they had at hand. We returned their enthusiasm. Our excitement grew with the decreasing distance to dry land.

A little before the agreed time, a motorboat made towards us. Both of us were busy with a final cleaning of NEVEREST and at first we did not see it. The next moment we heard excited exclamations and we saw Lara and my mother jumping up and waving at us excitedly from the deck of the approaching boat. A wave of unearthly joy swept over me. I'd never felt such a strong thrill before. Both were shouting at the tops of their voices: "Bulgarian heroes!" jumping and waving and their faces were lit up with the widest, most beautiful smiles. We began shouting and jumping on the deck. At this moment every cell in my body gushed with joy, I began to realise what we had achieved and that we were at the finale of an improbable adventure. A storm of thoughts and emotions was raging inside me. I kept repeating to myself that this was the finale, while jumping and shouting. I turned to my father and hugged him in the closest embrace that I could manage. We'd succeeded. Together. We lit a red and a white flare each and waved them above our heads. The boat with mum and Lara circled round us. This moment was a dream come true.

We proudly unfurled the Bulgarian flag above our heads. Although we could officially claim that we'd finished our voyage, we still hadn't yet stepped on dry land and we insisted on doing this without any outside help.

We were less than 2 nautical miles (3.7 kilometres) from land and we set out to row towards it. The motorboat captain however, announced that the border officials had warned him not to allow us to stop anywhere on the island before we'd passed through the immigration and medical controls at the port.

At this moment a wind blew up from the shore and gradually began to strengthen. Black clouds gathered over our heads and it began to rain. If things carried on this way, we wouldn't be able to get ashore by ourselves. We asked the motorboat captain to circle back with my mother and sister and then to come and take us in an hour's time. Fortunately, he turned out to be reasonable and disappeared behind the nearby headland while my father and I began rowing with all our strength towards the shore, changing over every 15 minutes.

Soon we were just metres away from a sandy beach, strewn here and there with rocks. We turned on the camera above the deck and jumped into the water which reached our waists. I was so dazed by what had happened, that when I jumped from the boat I stumbled and splashed into the water. We ran towards dry land and stepped onto the sandy beach, feeling the hard surface beneath our feet. We were intoxicated with joy and excitement. Up to the last moment of this voyage, we weren't sure if we'd manage to finish it. In my heart pride at the successful ending to this expedition, a first for Bulgaria, was mixed with relief and joy that I'd returned to my favourite people and civilization. At this moment the rain and wind stopped and the clouds above us began to disperse in sync with the final worries about berthing the boat. We staggered like drunkards on the sandy beach. The earth rocked under our feet. They say that sailors feel 'landsick' when they step on dry land after a long journey. Each of us managed to grab hold of a rock and we rushed to save NEVEREST, before the surf broke her on the rocks.

The Bulgarian ocean rowing boat NEVEREST arrived safe and sound in Barbados at 12 pm local time on the 6th of October 2020, after travelling 4444 nautical miles (8230 kilometres) for 105 days in the ocean. Each of us had done more than a million oar strokes. My father had lost exactly 10 kilograms in weight and I, 14 kilograms.

Bulgaria now has its First Ocean Rowing Expedition.

When we set out on the 14th of June 2020 from Portimão, Portugal, I was just 16 years and 293 days old, which makes me "The youngest person to row any ocean" and "The youngest person to row any ocean in a pair" official records, adjudicated by the Ocean Rowing Society and the Guinness Book of World Records.

Guinness World Records notes that "It was the first recorded row across the Atlantic east to west entirely within the hurricane season".

Later we realised that 2020 was the year with the most active tropical storms and hurricanes in the Atlantic Ocean, since official statistics began in 1851. In the 2020 hurricane season 30 named storms had developed, 13 of which were hurricanes and we had encountered four storms and one hurricane.

When I look back on this adventure, I think that the basic reasons for us to embark on it were to get to know our own capabilities, to sate our insatiable hunger for challenges, to spend time with each other, to serve a life-saving cause. I think that this voyage changed and enriched both of us. It was an invaluable lesson in growing up, no matter what the age.

There is no better way to bring to the fore both the good and bad sides of your character, than to put to the test every cell of your being. To provoke, to leave your comfort zone and there amidst the ocean of questions, emotions and difficulties, to understand who you are and what you can achieve. I did it and I know there are more oceans and challenges that await me. I know that I have people by my side, with whom I can go to the end of the world, without worrying about the unknown.

POSTSCRIPT

STEFAN

Almost every idea which at first seems impossible can be accomplished if you apply sufficient thought, preparation and effort to it. Random factors sometimes help, at other times hinder and no matter how much you prepare you'll still encounter unforeseen obstacles and pleasant surprises along the way. They make the whole experience still more exciting and unforgettable. After you have reached the finale, you're even pleased that there were more obstacles in your way than at first you could ever have foreseen.

We discovered that the bigger the obstacle you come up against, the more your mind and body summons the energy and willpower to help you cope with it. Then more people appear, more than you'd have expected – friends and strangers, who get down to helping with the realisation of the idea.

Everyday life to a large extent, follows a certain routine. Our job, friendship circle, way of life, family circumstances, etc. force us onto a path which we might not leave until the end of our days. When you take on a task which has nothing to do with your everyday activities, it's as if you've been reborn, as if you are discovering a new world with wonderful new dimensions, knowledge and emotions. You noticeably feel how you grow with every step of the task, how you gain confidence, strength and experience. Life becomes more interesting, exciting and unforgettable. You can even feel Zen.

When you immerse yourself in nature and feel it with every sense, you understand the true magnitude and beauty it possesses. The elements are frightening, but at the same time soul-shaking, alive and awe inspiring. You can't describe them adequately or recreate them realistically either in words or with photos and films. The actual feeling of being in the middle of a hurricane is not the same as watching a recording of it.

In times of adversity, the bonds that you build with those closest to you become even stronger. You meet new and unique people from other walks of life, whom otherwise you would never meet, let alone slip into their world or invite them into yours. What's better than to discover new friends and have them close to you?

To stop thinking and focusing only on yourself for a moment, to be selfless and show kindness to neighbours and strangers is like bestowing life. Yes! To life!

ACKNOWLEDGEMENTS

WARM AND HUMBLE THANKS

We would not have been able to start, let alone finish the Atlantic crossing in our little rowing boat without the guidance and support of the following people (in chronological order): Eugenia (Jenny) Ivanova, Phil Morrison, Nikolay Djambazov, Stoyan Voivodov, Victoria Dimitrova, Yuri Atanasov, Rumyana and Svilen Neykov, Emil Kiossev, Mylène Paquette, Pavel and Jordan Mihaylov, Maxim Behar, Terry Daniels, Kalin Dimitrov, Tanya Djachkova, Kremena Peneva, Kolio Bozakov, Valeri Petrov, Ralph Tuijn, David Matelicani and many others.

We give heartfelt thanks to everyone at Max's school, St. George's International School & Preschool in Sofia, who with incredible patience, supported and encouraged his crazy undertaking to cross the Atlantic in an ocean rowing boat during that unusual COVID summer! They lived through the adventure alongside us from beginning to end and sent us numberless messages and good wishes. Max was met enthusiastically by all the pupils and was rewarded with a medal for bravery and honour by the CEO, Kremena Peneva. The school organised on its own initiative a press conference and a party for over 200 of our friends and Max's fellow pupils, so we could tell of our experiences on the expedition.

We'd like to share that Jenny is our dream come true as a spouse and mother! Despite the fact that down to the last minute, she didn't know whether to let us launch into the ocean, she supported us with love and dedication from beginning to end and as the manager of the land based team, she organised the food, logistics, communications, material for the media and social networks, along with innumerable other tasks, without whose completion the expedition would not have arrived at its successful conclusion!

Jenny and Max's two Grannies – Karina Dimitrova and Zoya Sofronieva had thought of all the possible and impossible disasters which could befall us and with their endless pieces of caring advice helped us avoid a number of them – sunstroke, lack of sleep, sea predators, etc. as well as enjoy things to which we might forget to pay attention!

Max's sister, Lara Ivanova, helped us in the building of the boat on her own initiative and from the bottom of her heart. Together with our Grandads, father, sister, brother, father-in-law, sister-in-law, aunts, uncles, nephews and nieces, cousins and the remaining members of our family she was part of the most supportive family that a person could dream of.

We were overjoyed that old friends and unknown well-wishers sent us gigawatts of positive energy which pushed us forward from the beginning to the end of our voyage and beyond!

Our humble thanks to all!

We hope that your dreams too will come true and we are here to help with whatever we can!

We love what we do, and we'd love you to be a part of it.

Join us at www.vakon.bg or follow us on
Facebook vakonpublishing
Instagram vakonpublishing
vakon@vakon.bg